ONE STUDEN
SERVING GOD AND

D0728872

it's n~~o~~t easy being green

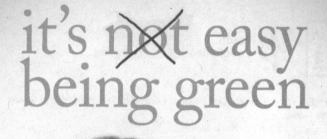

emma sleeth

 ZONDERVAN®

ZONDERVAN.com/
AUTHORTRACKER
follow your favorite authors

youth
specialties

It's Easy Being Green: One Student's Guide to Serving God and Saving the Planet
Copyright 2008 by Emma Sleeth

Youth Specialties products, 300 S. Pierce St., El Cajon, CA 92020 are published by Zondervan, 5300 Patterson Ave. SE, Grand Rapids, MI 49530.

Library of Congress Cataloging-in-Publication Data

Sleeth, Emma.
  It's easy being green : one student's guide to serving God and saving the planet / by Emma Sleeth.
      p. cm.
  Includes bibliographical references.
  ISBN 978-0-310-27925-9
  1. Human ecology—Religious aspects—Christianity. 2. Christian teenagers—Conduct of life. I. Title.
  BT695.5.S535 2008
  261.8'8—dc22

                                                                    2007045572

All Scripture quotations, unless otherwise indicated, are taken from the *Holy Bible, Today's New International Version™*. TNIV®. Copyright 2001, 2005 by International Bible Society. Used by permission of Zondervan. All rights reserved.

All rights reserved. No part of this publication may be reproduced, stored in a retrieval system, or transmitted in any form or by any means — electronic, mechanical, photocopy, recording, or any other — except for brief quotations in printed reviews, without the prior permission of the publisher.

Cover design by Toolbox Studios
Interior design by David Conn

Printed in the United States of America

---

08 09 10 11 12 • 17 16 15 14 13 12 11 10 9 8 7 6 5 4 3 2 1

To Mom

You are the best friend a daughter
could ever hope to have.

contents

acknowledgments

"Thank you" doesn't seem adequate when I think of all the wonderful people who have contributed in different ways to this book.

Clark: You've always inspired me. When you're out saving the world, I hope you'll still have time to hang out with your little sister and read "sci-fi poetry" together.

Dad: Anne of Green Gables says, "Imitation is the highest form of flattery." Look at the subtitle on this book. 'Nuff said. All I've ever wanted is to be you when I grow up.

Mom: I love you. Thank you for giving me a passion for language; thank you for all the books you read to me as a little kid—and even as a big kid every once in a while; thank you for all the hours you've spent helping me refine my writing skills. You've been the best editor, encourager, and guide I could ever have had during the creation of this book.

Hannah: You're a little glimpse of heaven to me. You are the most sincere person I've ever met. Thanks for teaching me how to communicate more clearly.

Dr. Spicer: Thank you for being like a second dad to me. For a person who says he has such an aversion to writing, you sure did help me out a lot during some of the hardest times I had finishing this book.

The Plumley family: You guys were there for all of it. Thanks for reading through the first drafts, letting me bounce ideas off you, encouraging me, and inviting me into your home. Oh, and Chris: Sara and I (combined) *will* beat you at Scattergories one of these days.

UBC and my amazing faith group: Thanks for the hugs, prayers, and encouragement.

McCarthy: Your English class—and, even more, your friendship—has changed my life.

Friends and faculty of St. Johnsbury Academy: The dedication and commitment of the SJA community is like nothing else I've ever encountered. Thank you. I think I'm safe in saying this is probably the latest an AOI research paper has ever been turned in.

Jenny: I know you didn't know what you were getting yourself into when you decided to room with me. Thank you for loving me unconditionally and inspiring me to live my life for Christ a little bit more fully every day.

All my teachers, mentors, and friends at Asbury College: You are amazing. Every class, every conversation, every chapel has been a blessing and a reminder that whatever I do—be it writing or recycling—should be for the glory of God.

Doug and all my other friends at Zondervan: Thank you for putting up with me while I was learning the ropes. You've taught me so much, and not just about editing.

Every friend who's mentioned in the pages of this book: Thank you for letting me hold you up as living examples of people dedicated to God and his creation. You are in my words because you are in my heart.

And Jesus: Thank you. You are the author of my life. You are my Savior. You are my friend. You are my all in all.

chapter 1

won't you be my neighbor?

E verything in life suddenly seems funnier when you have 17 people sitting on top of you.

About two years ago, a student in one of my mom's English classes—my mom's a teacher—started a "by teens, for teens" worship service. Every weekend we meet at Jamie's church on Sunday afternoon to sing, hear the Word, pray, and fellowship together. Jamie always plans some kind of activity to illustrate each of his mini-sermons: We've played thumb wars, lit matches, done push-ups (okay, *tried* to do push-ups in my case), and put together puzzles. But by far the most outrageous—and fun—activity Jamie ever had us do was musical chairs, love-your-neighbor style.

Jamie told each of us to grab a folding chair, and we set them all up in a circle. One of the girls from the praise band got her guitar. It was just like when we used to play musical chairs at birthday parties in elementary school. Every time Brittany stopped playing, we would stop circling the chairs and sit heavily in the closest one. Then a chair would be taken away, and we'd do it again. There was only one catch: In this version of the game, nobody ever got "out." Each time a chair was taken out of the circle, one more person would have to share a seat with a friend.

At first it wasn't bad: My best friend, Hannah, and I would take a chair together or Geoff, Jamie's seven-year-old brother, would sit on his big brother's lap. But as more and more chairs were taken away, the seating arrangements got less and less normal. Strangers began cramming together, four to a chair. Then we got down to two chairs. When Brittany resumed her song, Jamie folded up one more chair. We all laughed, not really expecting he'd have us all try to fit onto one chair. But then the guitar music stopped. We all bolted to the one chair instinctively, piling football player on top of computer genius, drama kid on top of math team captain.

When we all toppled off of one another, still laughing, Jamie explained the point of the game:

"When Jesus was asked what the most important things to do were, he answered that we should love God with all our heart, mind, soul, and strength, and that we should love our neighbors as ourselves."

What did this have to do with being crushed like a very small ant on a very heavy bowling ball?

"First, it means we need to really have hearts and minds and souls and strength—we need the chairs and the music and all of you guys who showed up today in order to play this game. We also need to know who our neighbors are: As you just found out, that's every single person here. But most importantly, we have to have love—we need to laugh and have fun and appreciate the blessings we've been given."

In a similar sense, I believe the only way we can protect our environment is by following Jesus' greatest commandment of all. We need to learn to love God and others with every part of our lives. If we're going to preserve the creation for future generations, we need to call on God. My dad is always telling me that God gave us the power to move mountains—the only thing we have to do is figure out which mountains need to be relocated.

Following Jesus' greatest commandment begins with our hearts. We must have compassion for those who are suffering—whether they be Kenyan children who are starving while we Americans throw away an average of 470 pounds of food per year, or Honduran elders who are dying of cancer because of the toxic pesticides used on coffee plantations, or kids our own age in Thailand who are choking on the smoke thrown into the air by factories that produce our school binders.

We hear so much about environmental concerns that sometimes our hearts can harden. I remember when my best friend Hannah cut off a foot of her hair. I thought I'd never get used to it. For the next month, every time I saw her I was once again surprised to see gentle waves of brown curling about her ears, no longer able to reach into her customary ponytail. But after a while Hannah's short hair began to seem normal. Now I have a hard time picturing Hannah *with* long hair. The same thing can happen to us regarding the environment. The first time we read an article about the declining state of the ecosystem, we can immediately commit to recycling everything, picking up trash by the side of the road, and carpooling more. But then we can lose our enthusiasm. Soon pollution again seems normal, greenhouse gases and curbside litter unavoidable. Loss of zeal really means loss of heart. In order to make a difference, we must really care about the people a polluted environment is affecting—and the God who calls us to do something about it.

But it's not just about our hearts. To protect the environment effectively we must also have minds. We must educate ourselves about the state of the planet and where it will be heading in the very near future if we do nothing to intervene. We must have knowledge about God's biblical demand to care for nature.

Remember when you were a young kid playing outside and you somehow "didn't hear" your mom calling you for dinner? "Sorry, Mom, I didn't hear you screaming at the top of your lungs those, er, 25 times" seemed like a sorry excuse when she glared at you with one eyebrow raised and her hands on her hips. Don't worry, the God of the universe hasn't borrowed your mother's floral apron, but he *is* going to hold us accountable for what we do or don't do to steward his creation. With massive climate changes, a plethora of available information about how we are destroying the planet, and hundreds of Bible verses all pointing to our need to care for God's earth, saying "we didn't know" to God isn't going to cut it.

Jamie also pointed out that we need souls. We need spirits rooted in God if we're going to sustain our commitment for the long haul. That's where our generation comes in. There are a lot of great people who care about the environment out there, but they can't do it by themselves. It's great that we've developed the technology to recycle paper that's previously been printed on or to reform old aluminum cans into new ones. But if we don't take the initiative to recycle those things in the first place, they aren't going to be able to do anything. It's up to us to find ways we can make a difference. If each of us makes even a few small changes, the results will have a huge impact on our climate. Many hands make light work—many souls do great works.

The fourth big quality we need if we're really going to make a noticeable difference in the health of our world is strength. I'm not talking about physical, do-500-sit-ups-at-a-time kind of strength—although I could personally do with a little more of that, too. No, I'm talking about a determination to do what's right, no matter how fruitless or tiring it may seem. I'm talking about the kind of stamina it takes to go the extra mile for God, even when all you want to do is finish your homework (well, okay, maybe you don't *want* to do that) and go to sleep.

I am horrible about following through on resolutions. I'm the kind of person who decides she's going to stop procrastinating—right up until that next assignment is due and I haven't got around to doing it yet. Or I decide I'm going to be better about writing back to people quickly, but by the next week my inbox is piled gigabytes high. Every time I clean my room,

I promise myself I won't let it get messy again—and then the second law of thermodynamics kicks in. Hey, it's the thought that counts, right? Wrong. Getting our thinking right is an important start, but the earth does not register good intentions. Protecting the ecosystem can't become another failed New Year's resolution—like an exercise plan or a work ethic that fizzles out after three weeks. We need to have endurance, if we are going to change the world.

who is my neighbor?

The second part of Jesus' great commandment is to love our neighbor as ourselves. But as my teen leader pointed out, if we want to do that, we need to know who our neighbor is. Yes, your neighbor is the sweet little old lady living next door who bought the wrapping paper for your school fundraiser when you were in third grade. But your neighbor is. also the bone-thin child from Kenya, the Honduran grandmother with cancer, and the teenager in Thailand who's already acquired a chronic cough she will keep for the rest of her life.

There is a danger in defining "neighbor" too narrowly. At my high school, the same group of people is in almost all my classes. I don't have a lot of interaction with students in other grades, or even others in my grade with different academic interests.

When I walk into history class each day, it's pretty much the same gang that was in my science class the previous period. These are the people I see every day, the ones whom I share memories with—they are my scholastic "neighbors." I've always justified my narrow view of "neighbor" by telling myself there's a reason we hang out together. I mean, why should I hang out with people who don't share any of my interests, who aren't preparing for college, or are at a different maturity level than I am? Only one problem: This kind of thinking is wrong. I'm the one who needs to grow up.

Near the end of my sophomore year, a student at our school was in a skiing accident. He hit a patch of ice before a race and remained in a coma for weeks. I helped fold the paper cranes our school sent down to cheer him up when he was in rehab, but I felt terrible. I'd never spoken to Tony before. I hadn't even realized he existed: He wasn't in my grade or in any of my classes. I mean—he was a sports kid. He liked computers. He didn't believe in God. What would I have to say to him? Quite a bit, as it turned out.

The next year I ended up in one of Tony's classes. Still, I didn't talk to him; in fact, I didn't even know he was the kid who'd been in the accident. Tony still wasn't my neighbor: He sat seven desks away from me and we never spoke. A few months into the year, our teacher gave us some reading time. To keep chatter down, he sent us in groups to different areas—and I found myself sitting between Tony and Nick on a carpeted stair landing. You'd think I would finally realize that the kid sitting two feet away from me is my neighbor. But no—I didn't know him; therefore, he was not my neighbor. Of course, as teenagers with the normal amount of procrastinating tendencies, we diligently read our books for about two whole seconds. Then one of us made a remark about something in the book, which led to another comment...

The next day we were sent out of the classroom in groups of two, sheep among the wolfish lockers. Maybe Mr. McCarthy thought we'd be less likely to talk if there were only two of us? Although Tony and I quickly opened our books and looked up innocently whenever Mr. McCarthy came to check on us, we proved a commonly known rule of high school: "Where two or three come together to do homework, very little gets done."

I wrote Tony a quick note the following day to finish up the conversation cut short by the school bell. The next day he wrote back. Then I wrote back to him. By then we were in a routine—we both kept thinking of just one more thing to say. Though we didn't have "much in common," Tony, the-kid-who-was-not-my-neighbor, turned out to be a fun, interesting, easygoing person who challenged me to look at life in a different way. Tony turned out to be exactly what I never thought he'd be: my neighbor.

Here's my point: Many of the same excuses I had for never talking to Tony are the same ones we American teens use to explain our disregard for God's creation.

demographic differences don't mean diddly-squat

The first thing that kept me from defining Tony as my neighbor was that we were in different grades. As teenagers, we tend to do the same thing on a global level. We assume adults should change their behavior first. They should be setting the example; they're the ones who can really make a difference. That's just ridiculous. We have just as much power to follow God's plan for the earth as our parents do.

It is also possible to go the other way with our thinking. Even if we recognize that we share responsibility for this planet with our neighbors in the generation before us, we do not always acknowledge our responsibility to those who will succeed us. We sometimes figure that, if the health of the world really is going downhill, at least we won't have to bear the brunt of it. And maybe we won't. But our children will. And if not them, then their children.

The bottom line is that we are consuming natural resources at an unsustainable rate, and the earth's population is growing too quickly for the planet to support. There is solid evidence for worldwide climate change—melted ice caps, droughts where there used to be water, and record high temperatures. We need to face these facts now, while change is still possible.

When I think about the next generation, I think of Cole, the six-month-old whom I babysit. A simple game of peek-a-boo or blowing raspberries on the back of his neck is all it takes to make him smile. Do I really wish smog-filled air on him? Well, if I don't stand up for Cole, who will? He can't even say "mommy" yet—that makes "global warming" out of the question. We have a responsibility to protect the people whom God loves, and that includes future generations.

beyond sympathy

Just as my "feeling bad" for Tony when he was in rehab didn't get us a wit closer to knowing each other, pitying others who face the consequences of our ecological neglect won't do them any good. Emotions alone won't keep one ounce of greenhouse gases out of the air, pick up one piece of trash, or prevent one tree from being cut down. Saying we care about the environment, thinking about the devastating effects of our reckless actions, or even talking about the need to protect nature isn't making the hole in the ozone layer any smaller, averting poisons from our water supplies, or cleaning up our air. When faced with a polluted planet and a dearth of natural resources, our children will not find it comforting to hear that we *meant* well.

Think about the last group project you did at school. If you showed up empty-handed a day before the assignment was due and told your teammates you'd really thought about the project a lot and hoped it would turn out nice, you'd be sure to receive a few evil eyes. In the same way, God calls us to action, not just good intentions. The environment is a group project. Just "feeling bad" doesn't help anyone and, unfortunately, the consequences of our inaction are much bigger than a glare and a bad grade. Don't just feel: Do!

luther says: plant a tree

Another reason I rarely ventured outside my own social circle was that I figured there must be *a reason* I hang out with the people I do. I make up this fictitious law in my head that says, "Like attracts to like." Somehow, everyone figures out (subconsciously) what people they are most compatible with, and that's how friendships are formed. Yeah, right.

Maybe we find it comforting to think there's some reason the environment is a shambles. Who knows what God is thinking? Maybe he doesn't care that we're trashing the planet. Again: yeah, right. The Bible makes it clear that God loves the earth and wants us to care for it.

When my dad talks to groups about the need to care for creation, he's often asked, "Isn't this environment thing kind of low on the list of Christian priorities?" What if Jesus comes back today?

Dad usually answers by telling a story about the German church reformer Martin Luther. Apparently, Luther once gave a Sunday morning sermon about the second coming of Christ. He was such a powerful preacher that when his parishioners went home, they all started acting as if Jesus were going to return that afternoon. One man from the church happened to walk by Luther's house and saw him planting a tree. The parishioner was puzzled and asked the preacher a question: If he really believed his own sermon, shouldn't he be doing what he'd want to be doing when Jesus returns? Luther answered that planting a tree was exactly what he wanted to be caught doing when the Lord came back.

I'd have to say "Amen." If Jesus came back this afternoon, I'd rather be tending to God's beautiful creation than doing just about anything else.

ignorance is not always bliss

Another reason I felt like Tony wasn't really my neighbor was because I didn't know him. I was relieving myself of responsibility for caring about Tony as my neighbor because I'd never looked him in the face and said, "Hi, my name is Emma." Of course, Tony was and is my neighbor—whether I realized it or not. I still had a responsibility to try to make his world a better place—even if we'd never had a conversation.

The same is true on a global level. It's easy to forget our responsibilities to people in other parts of the world because we've never looked them in the eye. But the billions of people who are suffering—and will be suffering—because of our irresponsible lifestyles are not just statistics. They are not just numbers. They are people. They are children of God. They are our neighbors. Not knowing is not an excuse.

The other way I justified my ignoring Tony was that I didn't know he was the kid who was in the skiing accident. He was just another unfamiliar face in a room full of big, scary seniors. But the fact that I didn't know

Tony was going through a particularly rough time and that he needed friends outside of his former sports circle didn't make his need for a friend any less.

Maybe you've never given much thought to the extent to which we've harmed God's creation or what you can do to help. That's okay. But we do need to take positive action, and the first step is admitting that a problem exists.

I love playing with Zach, a three-year-old whom I often babysit, while people are arriving for my church faith group. Like any other wholesome, more-American-than-apple-pie child, he enjoys playing hide-and-go-seek. He always hides in the same place—a little nook underneath a certain table—which admittedly makes the seeking part of the game a lot easier for me. The hard part is convincing him that he's really been found when he's still crouched in his favorite corner, eyes squeezed shut and covered by his little hands for an added precaution. He's got, "If I can't see you, you can't see me" syndrome. And when it's my turn to hide, it's almost impossible to find a place in the amount of time he takes to count to ten. Like "l-m-n-o-p" in the alphabet for most kids, "1-2-3-4-5-6-7-8-9-10" is slurred together for Zach, taking less than three seconds from start to finish.

Many of us are similarly naive when it comes to understanding the ecosystem. Fortunately, we have the

Bible: God's guidance can always be found in the same place, just like my dear Zach is always in his customary hiding place. But one of the biggest problems with our efforts to save the environment is that we tend to want to do things *our* way. Maybe solar panels seem more interesting than hanging clothes on the line. Maybe we'd like to say we're environmentalists without giving up our favorite food or gadget. Maybe we want to make changes in our own good time instead of fitting ourselves into God's schedule. Like Zach, we may want to skip the counting so we can get on with the seeking. But we have to remember that, even if we cover our eyes so we can't see the environmental issues the world is facing, that doesn't mean there's any less of a problem.

location, location!

My dumbest qualifier about who was my neighbor was physical location. I told myself that only the kids on my immediate left and right in English class were my neighbors because they were the only ones it would be rude to not talk to. Looking back, I guess you could say that my defining "neighbor" purely by physical location was a bit of a "blonde moment."

I'm sure you've heard blonde jokes before. When I was younger, my hair was quite a bit lighter, so I've heard all kinds of jokes playing on the stereotype of the "dumb blonde." You know: "Why did the blonde stare at her orange juice? Because it said 'concentrate.'"

Jesus' followers had a lot of "blonde moments." When Christ told the disciples to "beware of the leaven of the Pharisees," they thought he was scolding them for not bringing their own bread rather than giving them a spiritual commandment about how to conduct themselves. When Jesus told Nicodemus he had to be "born again," Nicodemus asked how this was possible, since it's obvious a full-grown man cannot fit back into his mother's womb. We sometimes miss the big picture when we take things too literally.

I shouldn't think of the kid right next to me as my neighbor, but rule out someone else because he's across the room. We shouldn't define those we need to help—by lessening our impact on God's creation—as only those we know or those already born, ignoring people around the globe or across the decades. If I define "neighbor" literally—as only the person whose mailbox is right next to mine—what am I wishing on my friend when I tell her to "break a leg" at a recital? Literal could be lethal.

we're all in this together

I know that talking about serious environmental problems can be discouraging. When my dad first left his job as an emergency room doctor to focus on global health issues and protecting the planet's ecosystem, it seemed like all we ever talked about was what was wrong with the world. I'd often storm away from the dinner table, overwhelmed by these doomsday discussions. I felt helpless and depressed. I have since learned, though, that the primary reason I couldn't stand to hear any more talk about the state of our planet was because I was focusing only on the problems, not on solutions.

I do not want you to get discouraged. While I believe it's imperative that we discuss the serious environmental issues we're facing, I also know that mulling over the problems of this world is not the way we're going to fix them. The situation we face is challenging, but not an insurmountable one. When we think about the beautiful creation our loving Father has provided for us to live on, our first reaction should not be frustration, discouragement, or anger—it should be thankfulness. Kermit was wrong: It *is* easy being green.

Often we can learn a lot about protecting the environment from people who have more positive habits than we do. I've learned a great deal about caring for the earth from my parents and their parents (and *their* parents). Mom is the one who taught me to garden and to can the extra vegetables at the end of the summer. Dad organized the recycling efforts of our family and took me to the recycling center when I was little to teach me how to sort out our reusable trash into the different containers. Grandma always let me cook with her when I visited, teaching me how to make "summer meals" that required relatively little heating time and "winter meals" when the oven could be used without heating up the house to unbearable temperatures.

My great-grandmother, whom I always thought was the neatest person ever, probably lived the most energy-efficient lifestyle of anyone I've ever known. She didn't own a car, lived in a small apartment that she wasn't constantly redecorating, wasn't a slave to fashion, and did all her cooking at home. She always turned off the lights when she left a room, which made her dimly lit apartment perfect for hide-and-seek. One of the things I loved most about Gram-Gram was her refusal to buy premade and overly packaged food. My favorite part of meals at her place was dessert, when we'd open the freezer to search for the homemade ice-cream sandwiches she'd prepared and tucked away in different corners of her freezer. It was like Easter all year round!

In the following pages, you'll find lots of suggestions for how to lessen your own environmental footprint (a fancy word for a measurement of the impact we have on nature). I am aware that this book is not comprehensive and that there are a lot of other great resources out there to help you in your journey to a greener lifestyle. Yet it's my attempt to pass along what I've learned at the ripe old age of 15—my own gardening or summer recipes or homemade ice-cream sandwiches. It's also my acknowledgment that the only way we can make a real difference is if we all pitch in. The environment isn't going to be saved by everyone talking about change, nor by a few individuals making radical shifts in the way they live. The challenge will be met only if everyone makes positive changes in their own patterns and habits. The planet needs individuals taking individual actions; small steps by millions of people equal big results. We're all responsible—we're all in this together.

> Throughout this book you'll find boxes like this with practical suggestions to help you care for God's creation. Pick the ones that work for you—and make the earth a greener place!

Throughout this book you'll find lots of practical suggestions for how you can green up your life. You'll find all kinds of ideas in the main chapters, but you'll also find a ton of practical suggestions scattered throughout the book in little boxes like the one on this page. Some of the tips are easy to do; others will take more effort. But remember: Every change you make toward a more earth-friendly way of living contributes to the healing of God's creation.

wrapping it up

Protecting the environment is part of what it means to love God with our heart, mind, soul, and strength, and to love our neighbors as ourselves. We can't say we love God and others and then continue to live in ways that destroy God's creation, lead to great human suffering, and endanger our planet.

God calls us to find creative ways to live that show care for his creation. I think that requires the kind of imagination I see in Zach, my little hide-and-seek buddy from faith group. Another game Zach and I love to play is basketball—without hoop and ball. We take turns running the length of the living room, bouncing our "ball" and shooting at our imagined net right above the doorway. We cordially congratulate each other on good shots, catch the ball for each other when it rebounds, and ask Cole (the six-month-old) for his opinion whenever we aren't sure if our form was good.

God wants us to play "basketball." He wants us to have compassion and zeal for people, even if we can't see

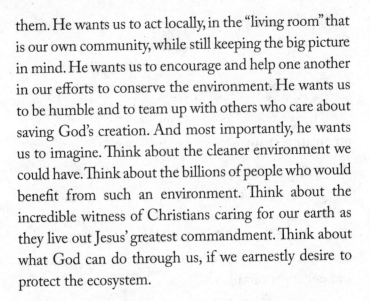

them. He wants us to act locally, in the "living room" that is our own community, while still keeping the big picture in mind. He wants us to encourage and help one another in our efforts to conserve the environment. He wants us to be humble and to team up with others who care about saving God's creation. And most importantly, he wants us to imagine. Think about the cleaner environment we could have. Think about the billions of people who would benefit from such an environment. Think about the incredible witness of Christians caring for our earth as they live out Jesus' greatest commandment. Think about what God can do through us, if we earnestly desire to protect the ecosystem.

Imagine serving God by saving the planet.

chapter 2

with great power comes great responsibility

I can be a real klutz. I'm not talking about tripping on stairs occasionally or dropping a piece of china every once in a while. That's normal. Instead, imagine a person who breaks her toe when she stumbles—standing in place. Someone who drops a water bottle that's guaranteed not to crack—and breaks it. That's me.

One of my most painful klutz moments happened in sixth grade. I've had many more embarrassing times, but this was probably the one involving the most blood and Band-Aids. It was at the beginning of summer vacation, and I'd just gotten a new scooter. Actually, the scooter was given to me *and* my brother, but it was my turn. For some reason, I thought it would be a good idea to go down a steep hill on the shiny new scooter with no shoes on.

Lesson *numero uno*: It is always hard to stop a scooter that is going fast, but it is especially difficult when one is not wearing shoes. The longer one hesitates, the faster one will be going. The faster a scooter is going, the harder it is to make the very sharp turn that is rapidly approaching.

You can imagine what happened. No, a life-sized action figure in a flashy cape didn't come swooping in to save me at the last possible moment. No, the laws of physics didn't suddenly stop applying, as much as I might have wished them to. No, I didn't pull a James Bond and use my handy-dandy watch with built-in grappling line to pull myself out of danger. No, I didn't suddenly realize it was all just a dream.

I crashed.

It was not a graceful crash. I scraped half the skin off my face, my knees were bloody and covered with sand, and I completely wrecked the scooter.

I should have known it wasn't a great idea to hop on my scooter barefoot and head downhill. I should have expected a crash because I know I'm prone to scrapes. I should have looked farther down the road before I went to the top of the hill. I should have known that no knight in shining armor would come to rescue me. I should have been more careful with the scooter, not only because I loved it, but also because it really wasn't mine to destroy. And I should have taken preventative measures, such as wearing sneakers, so I could've jumped off the scooter when I saw that things weren't going well—before it was too late. But I didn't pay any attention to the warning signs.

Copy one of the environmental Scripture verses from the appendix onto an index card and put it somewhere you'll see it often.

Right now, the way we are treating God's creation is a lot like me hopping on a scooter barefoot and heading down a steep hill. As Christians, we have been given insight into human nature through the Bible. The bottom line is that humans mess up. God created the world good. Creation was beautiful, pristine, and strong. But then we, through Adam and Eve, introduced sin into the picture. The Bible is filled with stories of human sin—disobedience to God, stubbornness, and self-serving behavior. You see, I'm not alone in my blunders. I come from a very long line of klutzes.

Yet even though many of us are klutzes, I think most of us sincerely want to make the world a better place. So why aren't we doing that?

One possibility is that we haven't looked far enough down the road. If there had been no obstacles at the end of the hill, I wouldn't have needed better balance or quicker reflexes. In the same way, our American consumerist lifestyles might not be such a problem if there were unlimited natural resources—all the clean air, clean water, and undefiled land we could ever need. But there isn't. God has given us a world with enough for everyone, but there are very real limits. If we continue on the path we are on, we're headed for a dangerous curve—whether we see it coming or not. We need to slow down our frantic pace, and find a new path.

Go to your school or local library and check out a book about the environmental issues that most interest you. (A few suggestions are listed in the back of this book.)

beyond wishful thinking

Many of us want to believe someone else will solve the problem. Maybe we're counting on scientists to come up with some whiz-bang technology that will save us. But that's like my wishing Superman would come and rescue me from my runaway scooter. Or maybe we think it's up to the government to do something about the direction in which our ecosystem is heading. But that's like my thinking I can turn off gravity whenever I please.

I am well versed in wishful thinking. I'm the kind of person who quickly scans her World Civ syllabus and thinks it says I have to read only pages 123-125, when I've really been assigned pages 123-152. If I wake up in the morning and spy a light dusting of snow outside my window, I immediately turn on my radio hoping to hear that school is cancelled. If I notice one morning that my always-too-long pants are suddenly the right length, I assume I've grown—never realizing that Mom just hemmed them.

It is easy to look at new energy-efficient technologies coming out and the promises of politicians and believe they really can save us. They look so much like the knights in shining armor that we crave. I believe our scientists and politicians certainly have a role in helping us find a more earth-friendly way of living. But the bottom line is that all of the alternative sources of energy in the United States together account for only about one percent of the nation's annual energy use. In fact, this percentage has actually gone down recently, because we continue to use more and more energy each year. Many politicians are only trying to get elected for a term, not to be popular for their conservation efforts a hundred years from now. Sometimes our knight in shining armor is only wearing spray-painted cardboard, as substantial as Styrofoam boulders in cheesy television shows. One senior at my school said in the yearbook, "I was going to save the world but then I saw something shiny." Let's not get distracted: The world can be saved if we focus on the right things.

I really did love that scooter and I felt bad about crashing it. But that didn't make much difference after it was a twisted, dirt-covered wreck.

I learned early on that saying, "I'm sorry"—even when I truly am—doesn't solve the problem. When my brother and I would fight when we were little, we'd both get sent up to our rooms for "time out." Eventually one of us would get bored and, after tapping the special "open your door" knock on the wall separating our rooms, would send a paper airplane down the hall to the other's room that would say, "I'm sorry. Make up? Love, Me." But even once we'd reconciled, we still had to go clean up the mess we'd made. Clark still had smarting teeth-marks where I'd bit him, and I still couldn't go on the outing my parents had forbidden me to go on.

It's the same with the environment. Saying we really love nature and that we're sorry we're harming it won't make the generation after us feel much better. What's worse, we won't just have to apologize to the millions of children who now occupy cradles around the world. We'll have to apologize to God.

Write to your local newspaper or government representatives about the environment. Leaders don't hear from the people who elected them as often as you might think—your voice really will matter. Be sure to offer constructive suggestions and praise any positive moves that have been made, rather than just criticizing or ranting.

There is a mistaken impression that God gave us this world to do whatever we want with it. Right after Adam and Eve were created, God said to them, "Be fruitful and multiply; fill the earth and subdue it; have dominion over the fish of the sea, over the birds of the air, and over every living thing that moves on the earth" (Genesis 1:28, NKJV). People sometimes think that because humans were granted "dominion" over other living things, that gives us the right to do whatever we please. But that word "dominion" really includes a responsibility to care for the planet. And in the years after they were expelled from the garden, more rules were given to the Hebrews about how they were to take care of nature, with specifics on everything from how to harvest a field to the humane treatment of domesticated animals.

The president or prime minister of a country has dominion over that country. He or she has been appointed to oversee the running of the nation. Does that mean these leaders can do whatever they want? All checks and balances aside, if government officials hope to be reelected, they can't just do anything they choose, serving only themselves and ignoring the needs, wants, and opinions of the people who elected them. Because of the trust countries put in their elected leaders, government officials have a greater responsibility to serve the nation than ordinary citizens. As one of my closest friends is always saying, "To whom much is given, from him much will be required" (Luke 12:48, NKJV). Or, as Uncle Ben from *Spider-Man* paraphrases the Holy Book, "With great power comes great responsibility."

Because we are God's people, we are "presidents" of nature. The Creator of the universe has elected us to look after the world he has made. Does this mean we can do whatever we want? On the contrary, it means we have a huge responsibility to care for his creation. The earth is a precious gift we've been asked to care for, not an entitlement. Just because it was my turn on my big brother's scooter didn't give me the right to destroy it.

Don't make the mistake of thinking that, because you are young, you don't have great power or great responsibility. We teens have a huge influence on our nation. Our parents are moved by our passion; younger kids think we are the coolest thing since sliced bread. We can use that influence for God. If we are on fire, the world will follow. Our generation is a generation that can change the planet.

wrapping it up

If I'd been wearing sneakers when I took the scooter down that steep hill, I could have stopped it before I got to the bend in the road. But I didn't take that simple precaution. Instead, I recklessly trusted that everything would go exactly as I wanted.

As a generation, we're hurtling downhill—and our bare feet aren't enough to prevent the crash that's coming. We're using resources at an unsustainable rate. We may not like nuclear power, yet we flick on a 100-watt light bulb without concern. We say we don't like being dependent on foreign oil, yet we don't give a thought to filling the tank with gas so we can go to the mall. In short, we may know that what we are doing is harmful, yet we are not taking any measures to change.

Fasten your seatbelts, friends. Or better yet, grab a pair of sneakers!

chapter 3

the places you'll go

From the time we're born, most of us are eager to be on the move. First, we learn to crawl, then we can't wait to walk, and before long we're riding a bike (or a scooter, or a skateboard) and looking forward to the big day when we get our driver's license.

Travel is not an inherently bad thing, and I certainly understand the urge to go mobile and see the world. Unfortunately, we often give far too little thought to the environmental impact of our choices involving transportation. Our continual desire to go farther and faster is leaving us with fewer and fewer beautiful and unpolluted places to visit. Let's take a look at a few ways we can be more conscientious about how and where we go.

vroom, vroom

Ever since the Model-T, Americans have been motoring around the country in their automobiles. Cars are an essential part of the American Dream, a status symbol, and a way of life in our nation. We have movies in which animated vehicles talk to one another, TV commercials that depict SUVs tearing across the back country, and magazines devoted entirely to racing vehicles round and round at dangerous speeds.

Lighten up your car. Don't carry unnecessary things in the trunk, and unload packages as soon as you get home. The less weight, the better the gas mileage.

Most of us haven't given much thought to our dependency on cars. I remember when Dad and I watched the James Dean movie, *Rebel without a Cause*—Dad had insisted I'd never understand the '50s until I sat through the film. The tape we borrowed from the library was a collector's edition with actor interviews, cut footage, and narration by the producer.

In one interview, James Dean was asked if he ever went fast when *he* drove, like the character he'd played in the film. James Dean looked into the camera and stated that he never went above the speed limit or took unnecessary risks while driving, because he didn't know what other drivers would do.

Only months after that interview, James Dean died in a car accident going 115 miles per hour.

Dean was lying to himself and to his teenage audience. He did not help anyone by his self-delusion. In the same way, though we aren't all getting into accidents while cruising in our Porsches, we tend to lie to ourselves about car-dependency. I don't have a driver's license and don't claim to know a wit about cars, yet I couldn't give up automobiles for even a week. Without a car, I wouldn't be able to get to school, church, or faith group; I'd have far fewer opportunities to hang out with my friends; and I'm not sure how I'd go grocery shopping or even make it to the SATs. In short, I need cars, whether I admit it or not.

Most of us know that every car on the road has a negative impact on the environment. But few of us are ready to give up car travel altogether. So what can we do to lessen the negative environmental impact of our addiction?

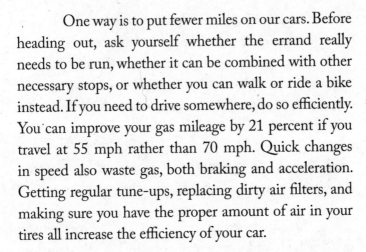

One way is to put fewer miles on our cars. Before heading out, ask yourself whether the errand really needs to be run, whether it can be combined with other necessary stops, or whether you can walk or ride a bike instead. If you need to drive somewhere, do so efficiently. You can improve your gas mileage by 21 percent if you travel at 55 mph rather than 70 mph. Quick changes in speed also waste gas, both braking and acceleration. Getting regular tune-ups, replacing dirty air filters, and making sure you have the proper amount of air in your tires all increase the efficiency of your car.

Carpooling is a great way to lessen your environmental impact. If you have a regular activity—a club, sport, or youth group—see if you can combine rides with someone who lives near you. It's also more fun. My favorite carpool was the one I took to dance class when I was in middle school. The dance studio was about 20 minutes away, so our taking one car instead of three every week definitely made a difference. When Jen's mom drove us, we would listen to different movie soundtracks—which is how I was introduced to *Newsies*, the classic girls' slumber party movie. Now what could be better than that?

Depending on where you live, public transportation may be an option. Is the loss of independence that results from riding the bus to school rather than taking a car really worth the respiratory problems exacerbated by vehicle pollution? When I went on a medical mission trip with my dad to Honduras, we met lots of people suffering from asthma—from little children to elderly people—who couldn't afford inhalers. We didn't have nearly enough inhalers for all the people who needed them. I don't want to make the air harder to breathe, especially for those who don't have access to treatment.

Biking is also a viable alternative. I am not the fastest biker. I distinctly remember going on a ride one beautiful summer afternoon and getting passed by two other bikers. I didn't feel too badly about the first guy. He was in his late twenties and was obviously pretty serious about biking—you could tell from his spandex outfit, his expensive road bike, and his calf muscles that were as big around as half-gallon milk jugs. But the second pass was embarrassing. There I was, in the prime of life, panting up a tough hill, when a 60-year-old man on an old rusty bike breezed past me holding on with one hand and eating a banana with the other. *Not* good for Emma's ego.

We always have people stopping by our house, but one of the neatest guests we've ever hosted was a bicyclist. We got a call from one of my dad's friends who said he'd just met a man in a coffee shop who was biking around the country and needed a place to stay for the night. Jim turned out to be a spirited middle-aged Englishman who pleased my mom and me by eating everything we put in front of him (nothing like a good eater to win over a cook's heart) and stayed up late talking with my dad about what he'd learned on his travels across our nation. When Jim rode off the next morning, munching on one last piece of homemade bread and jam Mom had served for breakfast, I was struck by how much better the world would be if we all took more time getting places, ate more home-cooked meals, and developed our muscles and minds as we spent time quietly enjoying God's creation without the constant drone of a motor doing the work for us.

And then there's walking. When I was in elementary school, Mom and I used to walk the three and a half miles to school one morning each week. Some of my best memories of those years are of walking beside Mom under falling leaves, during light snows, and on through the last few weeks of school when summer had come and the whole world was eye-squintingly and cloudlessly joyful. The other four days of the week, when I slept in one more hour and rode the bus to school, I often sat on the bus wishing I could trade that extra hour so I could enjoy every boulder, stream, and tree that were passing by my window as an indistinguishable blur.

leaving...on a jet plane

I always wanted to be an astronaut when I grew up. My classmates had their hearts set on becoming veterinarians, or nurses, or marine biologists, but I desperately wanted to become an astronaut. I read every book about space I could get hold of, checked out documentaries about space travel from the town library, and woke my parents up many a chilly night to gaze at meteor showers and rarely viewable comets.

When your family is shopping for a car, think small. Look for compact models that use less fuel. Better yet, get a hybrid.

When I was in the fourth grade I remember dragging a pillow and blanket underneath my bed so I could read *Contact* in peace and quiet, interruption free. Then, in fifth grade, came Random House's *Space Encyclopedia*, which I read cover to cover—a few pages each day during recess. And in sixth grade my dream came true: I went to Space Camp. My science teacher took eight of us budding aviators down to Huntsville, Alabama, for a week of camp. We spent the trip sitting in flight simulators, taking notes, marveling at out-of-commission planes, learning how to survive if stranded in a desert, wandering around the space museum, and riding in two-seater planes (even getting a chance to steer the plane ourselves for a few moments). Despite all the photos, life-sized models, and simulations, I learned the most just as I was leaving. I had some free time at the airport, so I wandered around the near-empty terminal. All down the hallway were displays about the history of space flight, featuring everything from fanciful imaginations from people centuries ago to Boeing helicopters that were still in the design phase. I stopped to wonder at a mural painted high above the quiet commuters who were just starting to arrive at the early hour. The mural spanned the wide hallway and depicted a huge flying contraption.

As I stood there looking up, a blue-uniformed stewardess paused next to me, tipping her head back at the same angle as mine to gaze at the imagined flying machine. "Do you know what that is?" she asked.

I just shook my head. Never taking her eyes off the painting, she explained that the mural was based on a sketch Leonardo da Vinci had drawn. He had been obsessed with flight, and had envisioned a machine that would make it possible for someone to fly, but had never built the soaring creation he had dreamed of.

I concluded that day that perhaps we humans were never meant to fly—at least in the unthinking way we do now.

Planes have their purpose. I'm not saying no one should ever fly. But we need to be a bit more judicious about our transportation choices. Many of us board planes multiple times each year, treating plane flight as nothing more than a convenient way to get from point A to point B, instead of the miracle da Vinci knew it to be. But planes are the most environmentally harmful form of travel. Every flight—whether it's a trip home over Christmas break, a semester abroad, or a Hawaiian vacation—has a significant environmental consequence.

I remember writing an essay on my freshman English final where I related the myth of Icarus to the science fiction book *Ender's Game*. In the legend, Icarus' father fashions wings out of wax and feathers that allow them both to fly, but the wings melt when Icarus flies too close to the sun. My essay was about how we often realize what we need to know, not when we are beginning a journey, but only after we have already started falling. For Icarus, the stakes were too high and his epiphany cost him his life. But Ender Wiggins learns what he needs to know and, by playing against the "rules" he's been taught in a military simulated game, unwittingly saves the entire human race.

Like Icarus, we, as a race, are flying too high in a very literal sense. The hundreds of thousands of flights that zoom across our skies are visibly polluting the air, making the sky less clear than it was when our parents were our age, and even changing the average temperatures in our country. Dad remembers looking up the day immediately after 9/11 and thinking the sky looked bluer than usual, more like the sky he remembered as a child. Later he found out he hadn't just imagined the difference. A scientific study found that in the days following the attack, the air was noticeably cleaner, with days warmer than average and nights cooler—because there weren't thousands of planes making trips across the country every day.

Use a permanent luggage tag instead of the disposable paper ones provided at the airport.

Our generation has a choice. On the one hand, we can keep flying too high and continue thoughtlessly harming God's creation with unrestrained plane travel and the pollution that goes with it. Or, like my hero Ender Wiggin, we can break the "rules" and choose to travel less frequently and less far. You don't have to step onto that plane. It might just save the world.

It is hard to get good statistics about the efficiency of flying versus other modes of transportation—since the figures vary with the number of people on the plane, type of plane, distance traveled, etc. Some experts argue that fully loaded planes are about as fuel efficient as cars, but the greenhouse effect of aircraft emissions released high in the atmosphere is three times worse than that of car emissions. Plus, airplanes encourage us to travel more miles—we don't drive over the ocean to Australia, or take a detour to Detroit when driving from Maine to Florida.

Maybe you find yourself thinking, "Yeah, but that plane's going to take off whether I'm on it or not." That's true. But "everybody's doing it" is not a good basis for making choices, especially as a Christian. God calls us to take personal responsibility for our actions, and do the moral thing, even if that choice is inconvenient or unpopular or seems strange to others. And while one person's refusing to step on a plane won't make the world significantly less polluted, what if thousands, maybe millions, of teenagers like you decide to make such a sacrifice for the health of our world? That *will* make a difference.

solutions to plane dependency

So what other options do we have if we want to reduce air travel? Biking and walking are wonderful ways to travel, but few of us have the stamina to travel across the country on our own power. That's not to say there aren't people who do. There are bicyclists like Jim from the previous section who ride amazing distances. There are others who walk, like the pastor's kid who once spoke at our school—he walked across the nation.

And then there are swimmers. Yup, swimmers. When I lived in Maine, the local YMCA kept a chart taped on the wall near the lap pool. On this chart dedicated community members kept track of the distance they swam at the pool—and lap-by-lap they "swam across the U.S.A." The chart included the various states and landmarks each swimmer had reached. It was fun to see if Carol had reached The Big Apple yet or if Aaron would be sending a postcard from Memphis any time soon.

Avoid using disposable cameras on trips.

No, I'm not encouraging aquatic long-distance travel, but it is important to realize that there are alternatives—and that traveling non-conventionally is both possible and fun.

But the biggest way to protect the environment through your travel choices is to travel less often. For family vacations, think about going somewhere in your state or "playing tourist" near where you live instead of journeying to other parts of the country. Consider a mission trip to an area of need within the United States instead of an international trip. If your extended family is spread out geographically, maybe the entire extended family could meet up once a year in a central location instead of everyone traveling separately to visit everyone else.

There is no easy way around the environmental effects of long-distance plane travel. The amount of energy required for plane travel has a significant impact on our God-created environment. This doesn't mean we have to be legalistic about our travel choices—but we should give some thought to the environmental effects of our travel plans.

"two if by sea"

On the day I turned ten, I became the proud captain of the *Millennium Midget*—a yellow inflatable boat I got for my birthday in 2000. The raft was five feet long, at most, and had "MM" printed on the stern in black type. Even though it took me 572 breaths to fully inflate it (yes, I counted), the Midget was perfect. I would take it down to the ocean at high tide on misty mornings and paddle my way from the public wharfs to the yacht club and back. I took it with me when we met my mom's side of the family for our annual get-together and floated it on the lake there. I took it up to Acadia National Park when we went to visit some friends. *MM* and I went to dozens of beaches and bodies of water over the years; each time she would shrink down to fit into a fabric bag that was tucked into the trunk of the car, and then she was reinflated with my 572 breaths when we got to our destination.

I never gave any thought to the environmental impact of the *Millennium Midget*. But I know now that every single lake, pond, river, stream, estuary, and ocean that the *Millennium Midget* entered is a little less healthy because I was there, a little less itself. On the bottom of my inflatable craft, really just a large pool toy, bacteria and invasive algae were given the chance to hitch a ride to the next boating site. In a new place where they didn't belong and where the ecosystem was not prepared to keep that particular species in check, the bacteria, plants, or algae had the opportunity to spread, disrupting the natural equilibrium of the body of water and choking out naturally existing species. Many lakes throughout the country are currently dying or being overrun with algae because someone—like me—has unwittingly introduced foreign species after boating on another body of water.

There is a very easy way to make small pleasure boats environmentally sound—simply clean them between outings. A simple scrub of soap and water, then drying with the bottom of the boat up in the sun, can keep invasive species from taking over.

Staying at a hotel on your trip? Conserve energy by reusing the same linens and towels for more than one day (just like you would at home), rather than having them replaced every day.

I remember during fourth grade when my school went on its annual camping trip to a Boy Scout campground in the middle of the woods in Maine. One of the activity options was boating on the little body of water we passed over every day as we walked between the eating area and the tents. One afternoon, a teacher and I were splashing around in a rowboat, a few girls from the tent next to mine were learning how to roll in a kayak, and some fifth-grade boys were cruising in a canoe. I don't know what was going through those boys' heads, but obviously it wasn't much. Apparently, they decided they could switch seats without going to shore. All three boys stood up at once, the canoe rolled back and forth dangerously for a few moments, and then the canoe tipped—dumping all three of them into the water. Mr. Brown and I rowed over and fished them out as best we could, and dragged their waterlogged craft to shore behind us.

God-centered environmentalism isn't supposed to be a killjoy. It doesn't mean we should never take a canoe out on the water. Yet we should be responsible. As long as we take precautions—as long as we go to shore before changing seats—we shouldn't end up falling in. Go ahead and enjoy the water—just make sure that it's going to enjoy you, too.

When packing for a plane trip, pack lightly. Every additional ten pounds per air traveler requires an additional 350 million gallons of jet fuel per year.

take the stairs, see the stars

Obviously, there are lots of ways to travel. But no matter where you're going or how you get there, movement takes energy.

Once when we were visiting my cousins, Mom took all of us to a science museum. One exhibit featured an exercise bike attached to a model elevator. The poster on the wall explained the amount of energy it takes to move an elevator up just one floor. The bike was to help visitors get a concrete feeling of what the numbers on the poster actually meant. As the person on the bike pedaled away, the model elevator would slowly rise. After my mom, my brother, the whole brood of male cousins, and I had all pedaled until exhaustion, we hadn't even raised the elevator halfway to the "second floor."

Ever since that day I have been loath to take an elevator if stairs are in sight. That's not to say such withdrawal has been easy. I used to love elevators. My brother and I always liked to try to jump at just the right time when an elevator going up arrives at the selected floor, since it feels like you hang in the air a second longer and jump an inch higher than normal— the way I imagine it feels when walking on the moon. But Hondurans need to breathe, and for that I have given up my dreams of moon walking via the elevator, and now use the stairs.

What do people in Honduras have to do with my taking the stairs? Let me explain. The first mission trip I ever took was to Honduras. The night before we flew down, our group stayed at a hotel near the airport.

Hannah and I were both jittery and couldn't sleep—I was going on my first-ever mission trip, and she was returning to her favorite place in the world. So we went on a little adventure. Wandering around the hotel, we discovered three staircases, all different. One had a trap door at the top, another was a squared-off spiral staircase that had an abandoned wheelchair at the bottom, and the third one was roped off with CAUTION tape at the bottom and was home to two overstuffed armchairs. To get some of our energy out, we raced each other up and down the vacant stairwells. Going down was fine, but on our way up, we couldn't breathe by the time we got to the fourth or fifth floor.

Of course, our shortness of breath that night was only temporary. I live in a place with relatively clean air that isn't unbearably hot, where I rarely *need* to exert myself physically, and where there are inhalers and medical care available if I require them. But the environment in Honduras is getting less and less livable because of our consumer demands, and the soil erosion and smog that result from growing coffee at an unnatural rate. The Hondurans I met on my trip work all day in this humid, polluted, hard-to-breathe air. There are no inhalers accessible to them; even when a doctor is available, there's no treatment. The energy that's consumed every time I take the elevator contributes to the deterioration of this environment. Is it really all that hard to take the stairs?

More than ever, we live in a global world; the little choices we make have ripple effects around the world. So this fifteen-year-old has decided to give up her mechanical "moon" walk so that the fifteen-year-olds in another country can see stars through the smog.

wrapping it up

No matter where you go, it takes energy to get there. With every journey you take, whether it's from one floor to another, one side of town to the other, or one country to another, keep in mind the environmental impact of your choices. As long as you are trying to honor God with your time and resources, you will be having a positive impact.

When I was at summer camp, the speaker showed us a few "de-motivational" posters each night to get us laughing. The last one was always a lead-in to his talk. One night the final poster featured a picture of snowflakes with the caption, "You're unique, just like everybody else." He used that poster to talk about the importance of discovering our unique gifts and purpose as part of the body of Christ (1 Corinthians 12:4-30). Another night, he used a poster about despair to lead a discussion of our personal walks. But my favorite poster featured a picture of french fries with a slogan that said, "Potential: Not everyone can be an astronaut when they grow up."

It's true: Not all of us can travel to the moon. Some of us will just have to settle for saving this planet.

chapter 4

meal time

I've always been a slow eater. When I was younger, I took great delight in eating pasta one noodle at a time, and I'd open soda cans so there was only a small crack to sip through. During the summers, my best friend and I would sit out on the porch eating Popsicles. We ate them so slowly that my mom had us keep Tupperware containers on our laps so we could catch (and refreeze) the half of the bar that melted into liquid sugar water before we got to it. I loved potato chips with ridges because I could nibble off one ridge at a time, making a game out of trying to bite off each one without breaking off part of the next.

But it wasn't just these treat foods, the ones it would make sense to savor, that I took extra care while eating. I found that celery was tremendously entertaining when eaten one curly fiber at a time. I felt that to consume more than one whole-grain Cheerio per bite would be to cheat the cereal of its full enjoyment potential. And then there was my chopstick phase, a year in which I refused to use any Western utensil so I could develop my Asian motor skills—just for the fun of it.

Yes, if I'd been allowed to eat the way I wanted to, I would have spent the whole day at the kitchen table. Fortunately, I have an older brother who prevented that. Clark has always been a tall kid—always growing, always eating. I can't remember a time when he wasn't a foot taller than me with a numerical shoe size twice as large as mine. Clark can pull the most plaintive puppy eyes in the world when he wants to—and he usually wants to whenever I have food on my plate and he doesn't. A typical meal during my childhood went something like this:

6:30 p.m.: Dinner served

6:31: Emma conquers fourth pea with chopsticks. Clark goes back for seconds.

6:33: Clark finishes second plate of food and returns to the kitchen. He grabs a rubber spatula to scrape pots to see if he can scavenge any more calories from their depths. Emma looks over at empty seat next to her. Her stomach growls ominously. Two grains of rice later she decides she'd better speed up, and promptly picks up her bowl to start shoveling in sustenance with her chopsticks.

Stow some fabric bags in the trunk of your car. Make a habit of bringing them in with you whenever you go into a store—to avoid the waste of paper bags or the environmental damage of plastic bags. If you forget, ask for paper instead of plastic and reuse the bags for collecting trash, covering textbooks, or as an alternative to paper towels for draining the grease off bacon.

6:33 and 20 seconds: Clark returns from the kitchen and looks longingly over at Emma's food. Emma looks up from her shoveling long enough to warn, "No."

6:33 and 35 seconds: Emma repeats, "Clark, I said, 'No.'" Brother continues to stare covetously at his sister's plate.

6:33 and 40 seconds: "NO."

6:33 and 41 seconds: "NO!"

6:33 and 42 seconds: Silence. Emma glances over at her brother, who looks at her as if to say, "How are you going to feel when my stomach is growling tonight, and you could have prevented it?" Emma's return look states, "Full."

Buy organic and fair-trade coffee, tea, and cocoa.

6:33 and 46 seconds: Exasperated and feeling guilty, Emma concedes: "Fine!"

6:33 and 52 seconds: Clark wipes his mouth after finishing Emma's dinner.

America is a lot like Clark at the dinner table of the world. While people are starving in third-world countries, their fertile farmland is being used to grow food that gets exported to the U.S. to fuel our nationwide gluttony. Not only is taking food away from local people in need unjust, it is environmentally irresponsible. It takes massive amounts of energy to ship fresh bananas to New England, seafood to the Midwest, and Ben and Jerry's to the South. It is possible, however, to make choices that will increase the environmental sustainability of our eating.

In third grade, we learned to do book reports by answering five questions about the story we had chosen: *Who? What? When? Where?* and *How?* Although unlocking the mystery of *The Hardy Boys Get Kidnapped…Again* is slightly different than understanding the environmental impact of what we eat, considering these same questions can help us make good food choices. Maybe once we hear the "plot" of certain ecologically harmful foods, we'll know not to pick them up at the grocery store—just as I knew, after hearing some of my classmates' reports, that there were certain books I had no interest in reading.

Pack an after-school snack instead of buying one from a school vending machine. By purchasing a larger bag of your favorite treat and bringing some each day in a reusable container, you avoid the waste of unnecessary packaging.

who?

Despite the colorful packaging of many processed foods and the impersonal environment of many supermarkets, we need to remember that food is produced by real people, sold by real people, and consumed by real people.

Does your family get take-out often? Check out which places near you use recyclable or reusable containers. Wash out plastic containers and use them again to store food. Some places will even let you bring your own food containers. And ask that no utensils be included in your bag when going through the drive-thru; instead, keep a few real ones in the glove compartment.

When I went to Honduras, I met some of the people who produce food for America. Many of the patients we saw at the clinics grew and harvested coffee. They came for medical treatment because of the diseases caused by poor drinking water, headaches from too much sun, and feet and shins that were chronically sore from the way they stood every day. The people I met there were sick and hurting because we want our cup of coffee in the morning. Coffee plants are very particular—I should know because I used to have one. (Note that I said, "used to.") Coffee plants grow naturally in the shade, under trees, at a certain temperature, and during a certain time of year. But because of the massive amounts of coffee the world drinks—and the desire to have that coffee cheap—coffee plants are being forced to grow in unnatural conditions. Entire fields are planted with coffee, despite the plant's natural need for shade. Because of the unnatural conditions, the fields have to be doused in pesticides, polluting the nearby water supplies and poisoning the soil. The topsoil quickly erodes, causing landslides, droughts, and sterile land in only a few years. Instead of working in the shade, coffee farmers harvest the beans with unbearably hot sun beating down on their backs, causing light-headedness and fainting.

Start a compost pile for food scraps and lawn clippings. When organic matter decomposes in the open air instead of in landfills, fewer greenhouse gases are produced. Use the nutrient-rich soil in your garden or flowerbeds.

This kind of coffee-growing reminds me of a paper I once wrote for American History. It was about how slavery was viewed at the time right before the Civil War. A few of the documents I cited had been written by slavery supporters who contended that slavery was good for the slaves. They received food, shelter, and medical care and were kept busy—work was something that the "naturally lazy race" wouldn't do on their own. Obviously, this argument is bogus: The slaves worked much harder than their masters and the food, shelter, and care were often barely enough to keep them alive and able to continue working. While the inhumanity of the slave owners in the South seems obvious, the northerners weren't much better. Because they wanted the economic benefits slavery brought to the country, many were willing to overlook the great injustices going on in their own backyard.

Don't use disposable stirrers for your hot drink—try putting sugar or milk at the bottom and then adding the coffee or using a metal spoon. Whenever possible, use a sugar bowl instead of individually wrapped packets.

Some of us want to believe that our consumerist lifestyle helps other people. We tell ourselves that developing countries need our business—if we did not buy from them, they would starve. I remember having an argument with a friend about sweatshops. She believed we should never buy from companies that utilize sweatshops and child labor. At the time I was convinced that if everybody in the United States suddenly stopped buying all products made from underpaid labor, it would harm the laborers more than it would help them, since they'd then receive no money at all. In other words, I was telling myself I was somehow benefiting people working in inhumane situations by purchasing these products.

Don't preheat the oven for foods that don't have to be cooked precisely—casseroles, lasagna, or roasts. When baking cookies or a cake, make sure the items to be cooked are ready to go in the oven the minute it reaches the right temperature.

Yet I don't think most of us are conscious of the "Who's" in our daily sustenance. We don't know the working conditions of the laborers who produced the ice cream; we only know we enjoy a scoop on a hot summer day. We don't know the environmental impact of the pesticides used to grow tomatoes; we only know the ones at the grocery market are less expensive than the organic ones at the health food store. We don't know that one type of apple has to be shipped from New Zealand while another is grown locally; we only know which one we like more. In this way we're a bit like the antebellum North: We want benefits without knowledge of our guilt. We may think ignorance is bliss, but every day we ignore these questions to keep our consciences cozy is another day that underpaid and overworked laborers must toil and environmental damage becomes more difficult to reverse.

My fourth-grade teacher had a laminated poster on the wall in her classroom, right by my assigned seat, so I saw it every day. It said:

> This is a story about four people: Everybody, Somebody, Anybody, and Nobody. There was an important job to be done, and Everybody was asked to do it. Everybody was sure that Somebody would do it. Anybody could have done it, but Nobody did. Somebody got angry because it was Everybody's job. Everybody knew that Anybody could do it, but Nobody realized that Somebody wouldn't do it. And Everybody blamed Somebody because Nobody did what Anybody could have done.

I think we are often like those personified abstracts on the poster in Mrs. Whelan's fourth-grade classroom. Every one of us can do something about the environment and make educated choices about what we consume, yet few of us do. We forget that *anybody* can make a difference.

what?

Jesus explicitly said that the most important thing isn't what goes into our mouths, but it's the words that come out of our mouths. But I don't think that means what we eat has nothing to do with godliness—

> Have a sweet tooth? Buy loose, unwrapped candy from the bins at the store if possible. If you get something in an aluminum foil wrapping (like Hershey's Kisses), recycle the metal by rolling it up and dropping it into an empty soda can that's going into the recycling.

especially in our day. Remember that Jesus was talking to a generation that had a very specific understanding about what kinds of foods were acceptable to eat. (They would have called a sausage pizza an abomination before God!) Jesus is introducing a radical new step in human understanding and relationship with God by saying that edifying words are more pleasing to God than eating the right foods. The fact that no food is inherently sinful to consume was an important concept for Jesus' followers to understand. Yet I think we always must go back to the Great Commandment to love God and others. And if we want to love our neighbors, some food choices are better than others.

One food choice you can make is to consume less meat. I'm not a complete vegetarian; if I get served something with meat, I eat it. But I do try to limit the amount of meat I eat. The horror stories I've heard about the way animals are treated in industrial meat production makes me glad I live where we can buy meat from small family farms. But I must admit that I don't avoid meat primarily out of compassion for poor little animals. No, I try to avoid meat more because of my concern for poor little children.

Get vegetarian dog food instead of meat-based products for your dog.

Let me explain: It takes a lot more land and water to produce the same number of calories from meat as from grains. Much of the meat eaten in the United States is imported from other countries that provide land where the animals are raised. If all of us ate less meat, that land could be used to grow crops that would sustain the local population. In many cases, native rainforests are being cut down so the land can be turned into pasture for cows. The people living in those countries are already feeling the effects of altered ecosystems—droughts, landslides, floods, and unusable land all result from widespread deforestation. Because I would not want my country turned into a desert so some teenager in another part of the world can have a burger, I don't think it's right for me to eat meat on a daily basis. I don't want to be doing to others what I wouldn't want done to me.

> Start a backyard garden. Got a Thumb of Death like I do? Try really easy plants like zucchini, squash, and herbs. Or, supplement grocery shopping with purchases from the local farmers' market.

when?

I love fruit. We have a whole raised bed in our garden devoted to strawberries, and Mom always bribes me to weed by promising me a handful of the sweet, juicy red fruit in return for my labor. But it's not just strawberries that I like. Blueberries, pineapple, oranges, apples, kiwi, watermelon, cantaloupe—oh, man, I could live on them. But I've found there are times when it's great to eat certain fruit, and other times when it may not be so great.

For example, here in New England, the fall is a great time for us to eat apples. While I can pick apples in the fall from an orchard less than ten miles away, it's very hard to grow grapefruit anywhere near where I live. Pretty much any fruit that we don't can or preserve ourselves from our own garden has to be shipped to New England during the winter. The fresh produce in our supermarkets during these months has to be shipped great distances. To sustain the journey, the fruit has to be genetically altered, sprayed with chemicals, and kept at certain temperatures en route. All this takes energy, further polluting the soil, oceans, and air around the world. Sometimes fresh fruit leads to anything but a fresh ecosystem.

Try soy in place of some of the meat in your family's diet—experiment with tofu instead of beef in a stir-fry or soy "ground beef" in a batch of chili.

Does that mean you should never eat fresh fruit? Of course not! But be conscious of when it is in season. Buy as much as possible from local fruit stands. And if at all possible, plant some fruit trees that thrive in your region. Speaking of your region...

where?

There are certain foods that make a whole lot of sense to eat if you live in one place, but not so much if you live in another. For example, it makes sense for me to put maple syrup in my oatmeal instead of brown sugar because the syrup comes from some friends in our church who tap their trees, whereas sugar cane doesn't grow around here, and thus any sugar I use has to be shipped from far away—and that consumes energy. Yet if I lived in the Caribbean, the case would be reversed.

Like popcorn? Get a popcorn maker and a large bag of popping corn to save on packaging and money. When going to the movies, get a large container of popcorn and share with the person going with you instead of getting two smaller ones.

Similarly, Mom doesn't buy eggs from the store because we have neighbors and friends who have chickens. It doesn't make sense for us to support an egg factory somewhere else when we can easily buy locally produced, organic eggs from Mr. Haskins.

The *where* question reminds me of a picture book my parents read to me when I was little. It was about a turtle with a toothache. He stayed in bed all day because he hurt so much. His family members tried everything they could think of to make him feel better, but couldn't. Finally, his grandmother came over to visit, and she gave him a piece of gum. When the turtle's sister saw him chewing the gum, she thought he'd been lying about the toothache—how could he chew gum if his mouth hurt? But the grandmother knew better. She asked the hurting turtle where his toothache was. The little guy pointed to his toe. His grandmother bandaged up the toe, and he was all better.

> When shopping for groceries, avoid unnecessary packaging and material that can't be recycled. Stay away from Styrofoam and most plastics. Buy bread that's packaged in only one wrapper instead of two layers.

The environment is hurting and, like the little turtle's family, we often feel like there's nothing we can do to help ease the pain. We know something is wrong, but we can't pinpoint the source of the pain. We don't realize that where our food comes from can be as important as what we eat. If we find out where our food is coming from and switch to more locally produced food, we can take a step toward healing.

how?

My mom is the queen of energy-efficient cooking. We've always had a kitchen cabinet devoted entirely to Tupperware or, as I said when I was little, "Tubberware." (They're tubs, aren't they?) Storing leftovers in reusable containers rather than using plastic wrap or tinfoil is just one way our family saves resources when in the kitchen. There are lots of others. Mom always tells me to precook vegetables and potatoes in the microwave (in ceramic bowls with lids) for a few minutes before cooking them on the stovetop because the microwave uses less energy. She puts any pots with leftover food out on the porch to cool in the winter before putting them in the refrigerator, so the fridge doesn't have to overwork to chill the food. We've disconnected the icemaker in our refrigerator because of the energy it uses when left on. Whenever Mom lights the oven, she tries to have something on both racks so the heat isn't being wasted. We often precut food before cooking—it requires a lot less energy to cook a stir-fry rather than a pot roast.

Mom cans homemade tomato sauce, pickles, and dilly beans from our garden so we'll have local vegetables in the winter. She buys in bulk and keeps the extras on a basement shelf so there's less packaging involved. This is part of her "pre-recycling" philosophy, which also includes not buying things packed in

Styrofoam, individual disposable packs, or a grade of plastic we can't recycle. We bring fabric bags when we shop so we don't have to get plastic or paper ones. (If we forget to bring fabric bags, we get paper bags and reuse them as trash bags.) And we have four labeled recycling bins beneath the shelves in our pantry so that our recycling is already sorted when we bring it to the center. Oh, and I can't forget the bag hanging next to the bins that holds plastic bags—they have to go to a different place than the other recyclables.

I can't imagine not eating everything on my plate—that's a habit drilled into me since I was little. We make sure any food scraps or inedible parts of a food (such as apple cores, egg shells, or the tough stalks of broccoli) go out to the compost pile. When these scraps decompose into nutrient-rich soil, Mom reuses it in the garden. Can you tell that my mother doesn't believe in wasting anything?

Many times the *how* of food selection goes hand-in-hand with the *who, what, when,* and *where.* I pointed out earlier that meat takes more land to produce than vegetables. But it's also heavily packaged in many cases, and then displayed on plastic-wrapped Styrofoam in open refrigerators in supermarkets. Since meat can't be eaten raw, even more energy and pollution is involved in preparation. Tofu is an alternative source of protein that takes less land to produce per calorie and isn't as destructive to the environment. It usually comes in recyclable plastic containers and doesn't have to be cooked to be eaten safely (though it's often heated). For our family, eggs are an even better source of protein. They are produced locally, take a minimal amount of energy to be cooked, and don't involve any throwaway packaging: We return the egg cartons to the farmers so they can be reused.

I once went to camp for a week up in Aroostook County, Maine—"The Potato Capitol of the East Coast." As we drove into town, the big sign outside the high school read, "Congratulations Jane Edwards, selected Junior Miss Potato Blossom, and Matt White, Junior Mr. Potato Spud of the Year." I didn't know whether to take it seriously or not. Then I looked at the meal plan for the week of camp. Home fries, baked potatoes, potato chips, potato cakes, mashed potatoes, fried potatoes, twice-baked potatoes, potato salad, potato soup, scalloped potatoes, potato pancakes, sautéed potatoes...it was a week-long "potato-cized" version of the shrimp scene in *Forrest Gump*. I didn't eat a potato for several years after going to summer camp in northern Maine. I guess there *can* be too much of a good thing.

Maybe you've given a lot of thought to the way your eating affects the environment and have already implemented a lot of the suggestions in this chapter. Or maybe you feel led to make a radical change in your diet right now. If so, great! But if the concept of eating in order to give future generations a cleaner environment is new to you, you might want to take it slow. Kicking a coffee habit for good or cutting down on the amount of meat you eat will make a much bigger difference than spending a week eating only lima beans, uncooked tofu, and water, and then giving up and having a near-allergic reaction to organic foods for the rest of your life.

Also, you have to be sensitive to those around you as you seek to change what you eat. Your mom or dad (or whoever cooks at your house) will probably be offended if you suddenly stop eating dinner because the meals have meat in them.

wrapping it up

Changing what we eat to protect the environment might seem strange at first, but it wouldn't be the first time people altered their diet for a social cause. I remember when we were studying the Progressive Era in American History and my teacher had us read little snippets of the literature and look at how that writing related to the culture of the time. In one excerpt from *The Jungle*, Upton Sinclair describes the gory and disgusting way meat was processed in his time. When I realized people had once eaten the gross meat Lewis describes (and often fell ill from it), I could see how meat grades were created by that generation. People were informed of the unpleasant facts, boycotted what needed to be boycotted, and finally changed the situation. But this wasn't the first or the last time Americans changed their diets to change the world. Think about the Boston Tea Party and the ensuing embargo in support of the war to win independence. Think about the victory gardens planted by countless Americans during World War II in order to reduce dependence on public food supply and support the effort to end fascism and Nazism.

Now, think about the out-of-season fruit that could be given up, the backyard gardens that could be planted, and the maple syrup that could be added to oatmeal in the battle for a cleaner environment.

chapter 5

dressing with style

The Bible gives us all kinds of information about Jesus. It tells us about how he had the power to heal people and even the power to raise someone from the dead. From the Scriptures we learn that Jesus told fantastic stories and spoke truths into people's hearts that moved them to change completely the way they were living—180-degree conversions. And the Bible tells us that, even though Jesus was the Son of God, he decided to die himself so that all who followed after him could live.

Yet nowhere in the four accounts of Jesus' life that appear in the Bible—what we now call the Gospels—is there a single word about the clothes he

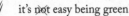

wore or the way he looked. Not once did any writer feel as though Jesus' appearance was crucial to who he was or what he came to say.

Now think about that. I often find myself describing people by the way they look—height, hair, and eye color. Maybe I'll even throw in a word or two about what they're wearing—a color that pops out at me or some distinctive accessory. Why is that? Why do we describe our friends by how they look but describe the best friend any of us has by what he did?

Don't fall for the latest trends. Buy clothes that will last and stay in style.

Now don't get me wrong: I'm a big fan of clothes. I think they're pretty handy, but only as far as they go. When Adam and Eve fell from grace, I'm glad they didn't stick with the all-fig-leaf wardrobe for very long. God gave them a gift of warm, practical clothing.

He didn't give them Prada.

He didn't give them Gucci.

He didn't give them Abercrombie, or American Eagle, or Gap.

My point is that I have a hard time believing God ever intended for us to be judged by what we wear or to judge others by how they look. Yes, God invented clothes. But he didn't invent fashion.

Next time you go clothes shopping, instead of hitting the mall, try going to Goodwill or another place that sells previously worn clothes. You'll be amazed at what you find.

When it comes to clothes, I'll admit it: I have a weakness for hoodies. Maybe that's because the dress code at my high school doesn't allow sweatshirts during school hours, so the rebel in me wants to wear them any other time. Or maybe it's because northern New England is a tad bit cold—summer occurs on July 26, from 10:00 in the morning until 2:00 in the afternoon. Whatever the reason, I absolutely *love* hooded sweatshirts. And I think we all have our little fashion fetishes.

But the problem with fashion is that it's not fashionable for the ecosystem. It takes a lot of resources to keep us up on the latest trends.

Now, I'm not advocating that we all go Britney Spears-style and skimp on our coverings. But in one sense, yes, I am saying that less is more. The less we buy, the less we consume, the less we feel entitled to, the more healthy and beautiful the world around us will be.

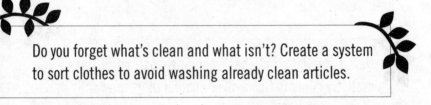

Do you forget what's clean and what isn't? Create a system to sort clothes to avoid washing already clean articles.

Fashion Tips

There are a lot of ways we can make what we wear less painful for the environment. One way is simply to shop less. It's amazing how we can step into a mall with nothing in mind that we need, and yet leave with a shopping bag or two in our hands. Whatever the latest hot clothing item happens to be, advertisers want us to believe we'll be incomplete unless we have one—if not four or five in varying colors. And that lie creates tons of waste.

If you're serious about lessening the environmental impact of your clothing choices, you might want to make a commitment to stop shopping altogether for a while. Choose a certain amount of time—six months, three months, maybe even just a single month—in which you will not go shopping. Tell your commitment to your parents and friends so they can hold you to it. Any reduction from your normal amount of mall cruising will help.

Another great idea is to make a commitment that you'll wait for some interval of time before buying anything. If you go shopping and find something you want to buy, put it on layaway or just put it back on the rack for a day, a week, or a month—whatever you decide. After the time has elapsed, if you still feel that your selection is necessary, go for it. But you may find you don't need that item nearly as much as you thought you did. Don't let sales and clearance racks deter you—if you went without it before, you can probably continue to exist just fine if someone else snags your bargain.

Use old clothes to make one-of-a-kind items like handbags and quilts.

Another way to make our clothing choices more earth-friendly is to buy secondhand or wear hand-me-downs. Just a few days ago I was looking through some family photos and saw a picture of my brother running through the backyard when he was eight years old.

"Hey," I called to my brother, who was sitting across the room, "I still have those shorts!"

Of course, it kind of hurt my ego to realize I'm the same size now as my brother was in third grade. But at the same time, it felt good to know that those soccer shorts had been in commission for a long time.

I'm also a huge fan of swapping clothes. My mom and I count it fortunate that we can fit into each other's clothes. She can always borrow a T-shirt from me, and when I need to dress up, there's always a skirt or dress I can snag from her closet. And then there's Mr. B., my sixth-grade math teacher—he actually had a co-op going with some fellow teachers in other schools where they would trade ties with one another, giving them a huge variety throughout the year. How cool is that?

Admittedly, there is some debate about what kinds of fabrics have the least negative impact on the environment. Although synthetics are obviously, well, *synthetic*—and thus not found in nature or easily reclaimed by nature—natural fibers like cotton and wool also take resources to grow and refine. For example, the land used to raise sheep gets compacted, making it less able to absorb rainfall. Growing cotton requires lots of pesticides, and cotton clothing often takes more energy to wash, dry, and iron than synthetic fibers. I've heard that it's better to buy either natural fibers or synthetics, but not blends—since each can be recycled separately but not together.

Mend it. Reuse it. Wear it out. Loan it. Give it away.

I don't pretend to be an expert on the subject, and I'll leave the details to the scientists. But I do know that, apart from food, clothing has the biggest environmental impact of any shopping we do. Nearly 40,000 gallons of water are used in the production and shipping of new clothes bought by the typical U.S. household—not to mention all the energy used to air condition and heat the stores, to produce the sale fliers in our Sunday paper, and to drive us to and from the mall. And we are incredibly wasteful: The average American throws away about 68 pounds of clothing and textiles each year—and about 85 percent of that ends up in landfills.

Wrapping It Up

One of the best gifts I've ever received was a tie-dyed T-shirt made by a close friend. It is my favorite shirt, but that's not because it's a particularly flattering color or cut for me. It's my favorite shirt because it has meaning. Dounia, the friend who gave me the T-shirt, painted on a quote from Shakespeare: "Virtue and graces in themselves speak what no words can utter." That shirt means a lot to me because she took the time to make it just for me and because she felt that quote actually applied to me in some way.

I am a firm believer that no one can improve upon Shakespeare's work. I am an English geek through and through—I have to admit, I've read *Twelfth Night* once for a class and around a dozen other times just for fun. And I think this particular quote from the Bard can be adapted to fit our world today. I believe virtues and grace in themselves speak not only "what no words can utter," but also what no clothes can say for us. In this image-driven culture, we need to remember God cares about the heart, not the hair. Let us be known by who we are, not what we wear.

We don't know what Jesus looked like, but we know what his heart was like. And that heart loved the world his Father created.

Check tags before you buy any article of clothing. Avoid items that need to be dry-cleaned, and seek out some of these greener clothing options:

Organic cotton is grown with few or no pesticides. Clothes made from organic cotton don't use chlorine bleaches or synthetic dyes.

Linen is made from flax, another traditional fiber crop that requires few chemical fertilizers, and less pesticide than traditional cotton.

Organic wool is increasingly becoming available; it is produced using sustainable farming practices.

Hemp is highly productive, easy to cultivate, and pest tolerant; its deep roots also bind and enrich the soil. It requires no agrichemicals to grow.

Bamboo is one of the newest eco-friendly fabrics just entering the green clothing market. It's hypoallergenic, absorbent, fast drying, and naturally antibacterial.

Recycled polyester, which is made from recycled bottles, can be found in some polar fleece jackets.

chapter 6

detector gadget

I love the English teacher I had in tenth grade, even
though he's the classic example of an absentminded
professor. One of my favorite memories of him was a
time when I saw him wandering down the hall toward
his classroom, coffee cup in hand, just like he did every
morning. But on this particular morning he stopped
in front of me. Instead of a normal greeting—a "hi" or
"good morning" or even just a nod—he stood stock-
still, looked me in the eye, and said, "In this world of
uncertainties, there are always bagpipers."

Then he kept right on walking.

My teacher's prophetic pronouncement might seem strange. But you see, at my school, there really are always bagpipers. We have an incredibly dedicated group of pipers at our school known as the Highlanders. For them, piping isn't just a hobby—it's a way of life. They march in parades, go to training camps over the summer, and perform every year at graduation. They've traveled to Scotland to participate in international bagpiping competitions. They even recently convinced our headmaster to make Highland a credit-earning academic class.

If you've never heard the bagpipes before, let me attempt to explain how they sound. They're loud. There's a low-pitched droning sound, but pipers can also reach really high-pitched notes—and those are really loud. The bagpipes squeak when people are first learning how to play them—think of the way a boy's voice cracks when he's going through puberty times ten. Those squeaks are really loud, too. And these sounds follow me through my school days: The Highlanders practice below my Anatomy and Figure drawing class, beside my dance class, and down the hall from the room I study in. I am haunted by the bagpipes.

Don't get me wrong: I like the bagpipes. But there is a time (*not* the first block of your day) and a place (outside in the middle of a field, perhaps, but definitely not high school corridors) for them. But as my teacher says, amidst all the uncertainties at my high school, there are always bagpipers.

Ever heard of too much of a good thing?

One of the certainties of our current world is technology. There are always new gizmos and gadgets. There are iPods and laptops and DVDs and CDs and PSPs and mp3s and cell phones and plasma screens and…the list just continues to grow. In this world there are always new technologies. And the way we relate to them has a huge effect on the environment.

Turn off your computer at night or whenever you won't be using it.

I am possibly the least tech-savvy teen in North America. I literally can't turn on my brother's computer. Of course, that may be because my brother built the computer himself using parts from several salvaged computers with three separate operating systems—but still, I should at least be able to turn it on.

I'm also one of those people who believes talking to technological devices will actually make them obey me.

Mom: "Who are you talking to, Emma? It's six in the morning!"

Me: "Er, the toaster."

Yet even with my high level of incompetence, I still manage to have my guilty technological pleasures. My brother and I actually have a deal about certain mindless TV series that we like to borrow from the library. I won't make fun of his shows, and he won't make fun of mine. Moderation in everything, right?

As long as it really is moderation.

My latest technological "guilty pleasure" has been playing Spider solitaire on my computer. Random, I know. But because I spend so much time writing on the computer, I often feel as if I deserve a little break. And I spend most of those breaks playing this game. But I've realized recently that what I meant by "little" isn't actually so little.

Let's do a bit of arithmetic. I usually let myself play two or three games of Spider after I finish a page

Buy songs online instead of purchasing CDs. Rent DVDs instead of buying them.

of writing. Each game takes about ten minutes. During summer vacation, I've been writing about five days a week—with a goal of writing seven pages a day. I have about 10 weeks when I'll be free to write this summer vacation. So that's 50 writing days times seven pages per day—350 pages. But if I play just two or three little games after every page, that's between 700 and 1,050 games of Spider solitaire. Multiply that by 10 minutes per game and divide by 60 minutes in each hour...Okay, if you've been zoning out until now, here's where you should focus back in again. Because the bottom line is that I'll play between 116.67 and 175 hours of a mindless computer game *just this summer vacation*. It's like I've spent a full week of my vacation—five to seven complete 24-hour days—doing nothing but playing this little game! Imagine what else I could do with that time.

Use rechargeable batteries instead of disposable ones. Once batteries are recharged, unplug the charger so it won't be using any energy.

Maybe you don't play Spider, but you might be surprised how much of your life gets taken up by similar random things—and in our day, those things often involve staring at a video screen. Take TV commercials as an example. By the time the average American turns 20, he or she will have seen more than a million commercials. Most Americans spend a full year of their lives watching television ads. Not TV in general: just commercials. For some reason, a year of my life doesn't feel like a *little* time spent watching what advertisers tell me I need—it seems like a lot more time than I want to spend.

Replace cell phones as infrequently as possible. If you do replace your phone, always recycle the old one.

breaking the video addiction

There are things we can do—both to make us aware of how much time we spend with our video screens and techno-gadgets, and to make those "guilty pleasures" more energy efficient. For starters, you can make your television more energy efficient by unplugging it completely when you're not using it (or using a strip outlet and switching the power off completely). That will make sure there's no phantom load.

Another way to limit the energy consumed by your television watching is to use a small, energy-efficient screen. If you have multiple televisions in the house, maybe you could pare down to one.

But the bigger challenge for many of us is to limit the amount of time we spend in front of the television. One easy way to do that is to decide what shows you're going to watch and record those shows. You'll be able to fast-forward through the commercials, which will save some time. But the added benefit is that you won't have the same temptation to just keep watching when *your* show is over, because you'll never start flipping through channels just to see what's on.

If you want to go even further, you might make a commitment to not watch TV for some amount of time. Try it for a week, or a month—and get an accountability partner to hold you to it. You may decide to never go back. Another tactic is to ask your parents to get rid of your cable subscription. With the amount that cable costs every month, it probably won't be too hard to persuade them.

I remember when a man I respect very much shared his testimony at faith group. He said that he and his wife stopped subscribing to cable television when they bought a new home, so they could more easily afford the mortgage payments. They quit cable primarily to cut expenses, but he said the decision turned out to be one of the biggest blessings in his life. He told us that he used to watch all the Red Sox games, and found that he'd get angry when they were losing. I couldn't imagine this gentle and dedicated father getting upset, especially about baseball. I mean, if he could handle the time when his three-year-old sprinkled baby powder all over the house without losing his cool, why would he lose his temper over a bunch of guys getting paid a lot to hit a ball and run around in circles? But with no cable, he no longer spends three hours a day watching every Red Sox game, and he doesn't have to struggle with his anger anymore. Sounds like a win-win situation to me.

Looking into getting a new computer? Laptops use less energy than desktops and require fewer materials to make. Refurbished computers are also a good option.

In our family, we have a DVD player, but no TV. Some people go a step further and have no TV or DVD player at all. You'll have to decide with the rest of your family what changes are feasible in your household. But the point is to cut back on how much time you spend in front of the tube. It's not only better for the environment; it's better for you.

The same principle applies to the computer. You have to decide what you can do to limit the amount of energy (yours and the world's) your computer consumes. Anything is better than nothing. You might be able to say you'll only use the Internet for school research—and then stick to it. Or you might be able to set time limits and hold to them. If you're like me, though, you might have to uninstall games. (Here's where smart tech-savvy older brothers come in handy.) Or you might decide not to have Internet access at home and go to the library for online time. Or maybe you'd want to get rid of IM or an e-mail account. You'll have to decide what works for you. But every little bit helps.

a new commandment

Once, when Clark and I were over at our friend Greg's house, I picked up a book Greg's youngest sister had left on the coffee table. It was a cute book, explaining the Ten Commandments in a kid's language. Most of the commandments were pretty easy to translate: "Don't lie" and "Listen to your Mommy and Daddy." But what about the last one? Exodus 20:17 says, "You shall not covet your neighbor's house. You shall not covet your neighbor's wife, or his male or female servant, his ox or donkey, or anything that belongs to your neighbor." How do you communicate that to a child? The book's answer: "Be happy with what you've got."

This principle applies to a lot more than the houses, and spouses, and farm animals listed on Moses' stone tablets. It applies to the food on our plates, the clothes we have, the homes where we live, and the parents God gave us. God wants us to appreciate all that we have; to be thankful, not greedy.

We can easily get trapped into thinking we always need the newest and best of everything. Take music, for example. We don't need every piece of new-fangled equipment in order to enjoy music, and the planet needs the pollution we create by purchasing new gadgets even less. Our parents were perfectly content with vinyl…until tapes came around. Tapes were awesome until CDs came into fashion. Now CDs are being replaced by mp3s. Is all this really necessary? We're asking for more than we need instead of being content with what we have. It simply is not essential to always be on the cutting edge with the latest way of listening to music—or even the latest CD from our favorite artist. Until that new form of listening came out or that album was released, we managed to live just fine without it. We need to resist the advertising around us that tells us to buy, to feed the consumer market, and instead listen to God. Have you heard what he has to say?

"Be happy with what you've got."

wrapping it up

God doesn't want to deny you the things that bring you joy. I don't think God has anything against the small pleasures of life—whether it's listening to your favorite CD, watching a favorite show, or even playing the occasional mindless game of Spider solitaire. He's not a legalistic God that wants to burden us down with a bunch of little rules and regulations about contraptions we've brought into our lives voluntarily.

I believe God really wants to give each of us a bigger life, one that has less negative impact on the environment and more positive impact on the world for his kingdom. God's love for us and for our world is the only real certainty in this uncertain world. And the joy of serving him is better than any of our guilty pleasures.

chapter 7

home, green home

I started recycling at a very young age.

Behind our house in Freeport there was a little path through the woods. The path led right to a parking lot that was located between our school and a little general store. And in that parking lot, there was a huge recycling receptacle—the kind we New Englanders call a "Silver Bullet." You know, it's one of those big metal containers with windows for different types of recyclable material—and usually a bit of graffiti on the outside.

That Silver Bullet was a beautiful thing.

When we were little, Clark and I used to race each other down the path. He always won. But I didn't care most of the time, because whenever our destination was that Silver Bullet, I was the real winner.

Save energy by setting the temperatures in your refrigerator and freezer at the warmest settings that still work for your family. Freezers can be set at 0-5 degrees Fahrenheit, and the fridge at around 40 degrees.

Panting, we would wait until no one was around, then Clark would boost me up to the "paper" window. I was small enough to wriggle through the opening into the little room carpeted by newspapers, cardboard boxes, and magazines. We had to go at just the right time: If it had just been emptied, there wasn't much in there and it was hard to climb back out; but if we went too late, not only was it hard to sift through all the contents but somebody might see me through the window. We also had to get there at the right time of day: Too early, and the sun wasn't high enough to shine through the little windows to illuminate my searches; too late, and people might dump paper on me as they brought their recycling during lunch break or after work.

With my brother keeping lookout, I would scrounge around among all the recycled paper, looking for two things: 1) interesting magazines we could cut pictures out of or use for origami paper, and 2) cereal box tops—the kind your school can get five cents for if you rip them off and bring them into the school office.

The school receptionist must have thought the Sleeth family did nothing but eat Cocoa Puffs all day. Actually, we never ate them—Mom always went for the healthy, granola-ish cereals that didn't have refundable box tops. But we managed to bring in many dollars worth of cardboard rectangles.

Instead of using the dishwasher's drying cycle, turn the dishwasher off after the rinse cycle and crack the door open to let dishes air-dry.

From our rather devious salvaging escapades as children, Clark and I learned a few things about recycling. We learned that cooperation is necessary for success: Yes, I did get stuck more than once when I tried to go in by myself. We also learned the truth of the old cliché: "One man's trash is another man's treasure." And finally, we learned that recycling often translates into money.

Recycling remains one of the most important things you can do at home to help care for the environment. If your family doesn't recycle, start now. At our house, we have four plastic tubs lined up in the pantry underneath the shelves: one for paper and cardboard, one for glass and plastic, one for steel cans, and one for aluminum cans. Some communities make

Confused about what can and can't be recycled? Research online or go to your local recycling center to see what your town accepts.

recycling super-easy by offering curbside pick-up—you just set the recycling containers out with the trash cans. We need to take our materials to the recycling center, but we've found it's really not much extra effort. Whenever we need to run errands in Littleton, we take the first three bins to the center there. Whenever the fourth one fills up, we take it into the can refund center in St. Johnsbury. Recycling all these materials means we rarely have more than a paper bag full of garbage on the curb on trash day. Plus, there's the added bonus of being able to peruse the used book exchange at the recycling center whenever I go with Mom. One of my best Bible reference books came from the recycling center.

Composting comes right along with recycling. It makes so much sense. We have a pitcher that stays right by the sink to put food scraps in when we're doing the dishes or cooking. When the pitcher is full—usually about once a day—one of us will dump the contents on the compost pile by the side of our property. We've tried more complicated things like worms and different additives that are supposed to speed up the composting process, but we've found that our simple piles work just fine. Every few years, we just begin a new pile and add the decomposing material in the other pile to our garden. And because we take out the compost so often and clean out the pitcher each time, we've never had a problem with the food scraps getting smelly or attracting bugs. There's no lid, nothing added to the scraps to reduce odors—just quite a few apple cores and broccoli stalks that get taken out quite frequently.

Lighting candles or the fireplace? Opt for matches instead of a lighter—the plastic and fuel create more waste—and use cardboard matches over wooden ones.

There are so many things you can do around your own home to make it better for the environment. Some of the changes will require the cooperation of your family to maximize the impact, but you can start alone. Some of the changes may seem inconvenient at first, or too much like chores, but they can add so much to your life if you see them for what they really are: ways of honoring God and great opportunities

Use the coolest water possible when doing the wash.

to spend more time with your family working toward a common goal. Many of the changes will seem less onerous if you compare your lifestyle with those of teens living in areas of our world most severely affected by poverty and environmental problems. The worst "inconvenience" you encounter in trying to live a more

Recycle newspapers. Better yet, get the information online.

earth-friendly life might seem like the height of luxury for teens in countries like Honduras or Haiti, who have to wonder if they have safe drinking water or clean air to breathe. And I'm willing to bet that a lot of the simple changes you can make around your house will also save money—money that you'd probably prefer to be giving to a charity or ministry rather than an electric company.

Hang up drapes to insulate windows. Really like the sheer curtains you already have? Try layering them with thicker ones. The more the merrier!

a dozen suggestions for a greener home

Looking for more things you can do to make your house better for the environment? Here are 12 ideas for how you can make your home greener:

    1. One of the most significant things you can do *immediately* to lessen your environmental impact is to change the five most often used light bulbs in your house to compact fluorescents. Seems like no big thing, right? Wrong! If everybody in America made just this one change, we could shut down 21 coal-fired energy plants tomorrow. In terms of environmental impact, this is the equivalent of taking 8 million cars off the road! Like the other electricity-saving steps I've mentioned earlier—unplugging stereos and TVs when they're not on, turning off computers

when you're not using them, and just flicking off the lights when you leave the room—this is a great idea that doesn't take much effort but can reduce your family's environmental footprint significantly.

Set the thermostat higher in the summer (at least 78°F) and cooler (68°F or lower) in the winter. A programmable thermostat can help cut heating and cooling bills even further.

2. You can also change the showerheads in your home to ones that use less water. When my brother was in grade school, I remember his class performed a play before the whole school that showed how to be good to the environment. One little girl showed how much water gets wasted if we leave the water running while we brush our teeth. As she brushed, a classmate poured water out of a gallon milk jug into a basin to simulate the faucet she'd left running. When I was watching the skit, I remember silently urging the neglectful girl to "turn off" the water—the same way I now urge characters in movies to look behind them or say the right thing. It just seemed so wasteful.

But now I realize that the girl used up only one gallon of water in her carelessness. Just one. The average showerhead uses anywhere from four to ten gallons *per minute.* Multiply that by a 10-minute shower per day per person, and that's quite a few thousand gallons of water per week for your entire family. It's possible to find replacement showerheads that reduce the water flow to about two gallons per minute. Switching to more efficient showerheads and making an effort to take shorter showers both have potential to save a lot more water than that one girl turning off the water while brushing her teeth. (But go ahead and turn off the water while you brush, too—every little bit helps!)

If you're cold, put on a hoodie instead of turning up the heat.

3. Hang clothes out on a line to dry instead of using a clothes dryer. Yes, it does take a little more time. But when the weather is nice, it's great to spend time outside—either with other family members or by yourself with the birds and clouds. In the wintertime, you can set up

a line or rack inside so you don't need to use the dryer. We have a retractable line inside that goes the whole length of the south side of our house, as well as a wooden bar that can be hung up in front of the woodstove. We keep a set of hangers next to the washing machine specifically for hanging the bigger articles of clothing on the bar, while lighter items—socks, handkerchiefs, napkins, rags, lighter shirts, and my leotards—get hung directly on the line.

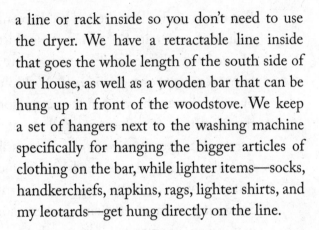

Do you have a pool in the backyard? Cover it when not in use to avoid evaporation and so that it will need to be cleaned less.

4. Speaking of the south side, much of our heat in the winter comes from sunlight shining through our south-facing windows; we only have one window on the north side. I know you don't have a choice about the location of the windows in your house. But you can decide to make those windows more helpful in the heating and cooling of your home. During the summer, curtains on the south side can limit the sunlight and keep your home cooler, while thick

curtains on all windows can act as insulation during winter nights. Curtains don't have to be expensive or fancy: One of my first memories is of my mom sitting at the sewing machine when I was two, making flowered curtains from sheets she'd bought on sale.

Switch to renewable energy if it's available in your area. It may cost more, but the planet will thank you.

5. Use rags, fabric bags, and handkerchiefs instead of paper towels, plastic grocery bags, and Kleenex. Reusable fabric bags and cleaning rags are so much better for the environment than disposable ones that get used once and tossed in the trash. And handkerchiefs are great. I don't get why everybody seems to think they are less clean than paper tissues; it's not like they don't get washed. People used them for thousands of years and were fine with it. If cloth was good enough for Jesus' nose, I think I can handle it, too. And the bottom line is that the world will be a whole lot *less* clean for our children if we keep using disposable tissues every time we get a cold. Besides, handkerchiefs are so much

more practical than tissues. Which would you rather use to tie up your possessions when you're running away from home: a tissue or a piece of cloth? When I was seven years old and decided to run away, I was very thankful my parents were old-fashioned enough to have handkerchiefs (but not thankful enough to not run away).

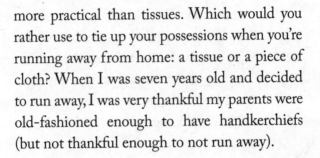

Call to stop having phone books delivered. You can keep an old one around and use the Internet to find any numbers that have changed.

6. Wash the dishes by hand instead of using a dishwasher. Some dishwasher manufacturers claim it uses more water to wash dishes by hand—but when my dad actually measured it, there was no contest. Unless you leave the water running the whole time and don't use a basin or stopper, washing dishes by hand uses not only less water but also far less electricity. Besides, most people usually rinse dishes before they're put in the dishwasher anyway.

I've found that doing the dishes is a total mind game: If you decide you don't like doing the dishes, then you won't. But if you do them with someone else, wash a few while you're waiting for something in the toaster or microwave, or just enjoy the view out the window while you're washing them, it's really not bad. My favorite time for doing the dishes is right after dinner—my brother washes, I dry and put away. It's a fun time to have quoting wars, decide how things would be done if we were in charge, critique the latest books we've read, or just see how quickly we can do all the dishes (without breaking anything). No, we're not the perfect nuclear family from a 1950s magazine ad, always smiling while doing the chores. But we do have fun when doing the dishes together—more fun than when we had a dishwasher in the house.

Wrap the water heater in an insulating blanket and set the thermostat no higher than 120 degrees.

7. Mow the lawn using a push mower and/ or let some of your yard just grow. Okay, so maybe some of the neighbors will frown. But others might decide to follow your lead. When

we lived in Maine, we stopped mowing the backyard after a while. We could still play in it, it was a lot less work, and it took a lot less time and resources. One of our neighbors didn't like it. But two others stopped mowing their lawns, too. When we moved and built a passive solar home, we opted for wildflowers instead of grass in the yard. We've had two people stop to

Talk to your parents about switching to paperless bank statements. When using an ATM, don't take a receipt.

paint pictures of our yard, several others have photographed it, and there was even one guy who knocked on our door to ask if he could pick some of the flowers because he'd forgotten to get his wife an anniversary gift. Plus, we get to bring bouquets to people all the time, and the retired teacher next door regularly picks flowers for church dinners and events. And—as my dad likes to say—how many other people can bring *their* lawn clippings as a gift when they're invited to come over to someone's house for dinner? My best friend, Hannah, once showed up at my house for dinner and gave Mom a bag full of

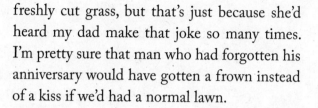

freshly cut grass, but that's just because she'd heard my dad make that joke so many times. I'm pretty sure that man who had forgotten his anniversary would have gotten a frown instead of a kiss if we'd had a normal lawn.

8. Whenever possible, use fans instead of air conditioning. Fans use a fraction of the electricity air conditioners use, and contribute far fewer greenhouse gases. And when the weather gets cold, turn the thermostat down a few degrees and wear sweaters and slippers around the house. You can turn the temperature down even lower at night and add a comforter to your bed.

9. Stop using unnecessary gadgets that waste energy. Unplug the icemaker in the freezer. Get rid of the lava lamp. Cut back on electronic games. My parents taught me to ask two questions about any decision: Will this bring me closer to God, and am I loving my neighbor? When I remember to apply these questions to video games, iPods, and Internet surfing, I invariably make better choices.

10. Speaking of unnecessary gadgets—gals, don't blow-dry, straighten, or curl your hair. Not only will you save electricity, you'll save time getting ready in the morning. Hairstyles

go in cycles anyway. I'll never forget when a girl at school suddenly told me she really liked my hair. I'd been going to school with her for three years, and my hair hadn't changed a bit. Only the styles had. I know my hair will go out of fashion again, but...vanities of vanities... now I can say I don't straighten my hair for *environmental* reasons.

11. You know all the junk mail that arrives at your house every day—the endless stream of advertisements for new credit cards, products you don't need, and magazines you'll never read? Well, you can stop getting it. Write to:

> Mail Preference Service
> c/o Direct Marketing Association
> PO Box 9008
> Farmingdale, NY 11735-9008

Include the date, a parent's name and address, and a note that says, "Please register my name with the Mail Preference Service." Make sure you have that parent sign the note. After a couple of months, if you're still getting advertisements you don't want, call any companies that send you their materials and say you would like to be taken off their mailing list.

12. Insulate. This is one you probably can't do on your own—but you can offer to help your parents with insulating projects. If your water heater is more than five years old and has no internal insulation, get an insulating jacket for it. Caulk and weather-strip around windows and doors. Even putting a rolled-up towel at the bottom of a door can help with drafts—that's the way our dance teacher does it. (She says she needs to keep the room warm for our muscles.) Even small measures like these can make a big difference.

wrapping it up

They say home is where the heart is—and home is also the best place to start in making our lives greener. In offering lots of suggestions for making your home more earth-friendly, my point isn't to make you feel guilty about all the things you *should be* doing differently. My point is to help you see that there are so many ways—some very simple, some a little tougher—to have a positive impact on the environment. We all have the ability to change the world, one choice at a time.

There are so many steps you can take to make your home more energy efficient. And just think about it: Not even one of them requires you to climb through a tiny window and drop into a stuffy, smelly, metal recycling compartment. You have it *so* easy.

making your holidays environmentally friendly

I love holidays—but the rampant consumerism that's so often part of our holiday celebrations is disastrous for the environment. Below are just a few suggestions for how to green up your holiday celebrations:

- Give the gift of your time. Make certificates entitling your parents to a night out while you watch your younger siblings, or make breakfast in bed for your parent on Mother's or Father's Day instead of buying a card.

- Start a family Christmas tradition that doesn't focus on presents—go ice-skating, read the Christmas story aloud from the Bible, or play a board game together.

- Reuse wrapping paper and ribbon. Better yet, wrap gifts in practical, reusable things—nice fabric bags or wicker baskets. You can also recycle Christmas cards by cutting off the front and reusing it as a postcard or gift tag.

- Avoid holiday decorations that light up or need batteries.

- For your Christmas tree, try getting a potted evergreen that can be replanted in the spring, instead of a tree that has been cut down.

- Instead of everybody in your family getting a Christmas present for everyone else, agree that each person will give a present to only one other family member.

- Going to a baby shower? Try getting a green gift—a baby blanket made of organic fibers or a toy made from renewable resources.

- Try getting a pretty potted flower instead of a cut bouquet for Valentine's Day and tell them that you hope your friendship will always keep growing.

- Give the gift of a better world. Instead of getting a friend or family member a trinket, donate to a charity or environmental organization in his or her name.

- Consider giving gift certificates to a local natural food store or membership at a co-op.

- Volunteer at a local charity or soup kitchen at Thanksgiving or during the Christmas season. It's a great way to share God's love, and remember our own blessings.

chapter 8

too cool for school

T his morning, my dad talked to a class full of
fourth graders about the environment. He spoke
with the class by speakerphone—one of my younger
friends from our faith group in the last place we lived
had set it all up. Erin was excited about sharing one of
her favorite adults with her friends. And that adult was
really excited about talking to the kids.

Now you have to understand: My dad speaks
about the environment all the time. He has meetings
with the head of the Sierra Club, preaches in churches
with 10,000 members, and rubs shoulders with some of
the most knowledgeable and influential scientists who
are researching climate change. He's been followed

by camera crews and interviewed on national radio programs. So you might not think he'd be all that excited about speaking by phone to a classroom of elementary school kids.

But when I came into the kitchen a few hours after everyone else had gotten up (I'm a teen, okay?), Dad was practically bouncing off the walls, waiting for the class to call. He didn't even want to toast his English muffin, because it might take too long and he wanted to be done eating when the phone rang.

When dad got off the phone, he said the class was awesome. He always says that if you talk to kids like adults, they'll respond. Nobody likes being talked down to, no matter how old they are. Kids always want to know, "What can I do? What can I do?" instead of wanting to change other people. My dad is convinced that this desire to work on our own personal habits before trying to get other people to change is what's really going to help the ecosystem. And he loved that the kids were all happy to comply with his request to give his young friend Erin a hug for him because he lives too far away now.

Obviously, it's been a while since most of us were in fourth grade. But as I think about Dad talking to Erin's class, I believe there are a few ideas we can learn that apply not only to our younger friends but also to us "big kids" in high school or junior high.

The first is that most adults really love interacting with kids—and vice versa. There is something exciting about youth. We might not be famous, we might not have all the answers, but young people have an energy and passion that is contagious. And when it comes to saving the earth, that energy can help get others excited about joining in.

Reuse Post-It notes instead of throwing them away after one use.

Dad's talk with the fourth graders also reminds me that there needs to be respect and cooperation across generations in order for us to have a greener planet. Dad didn't talk down to the kids, and when it comes to serious issues like the environment, we teenagers don't need—or want—some oversimplified "environmentalism for dummies" version. When we are enthusiastic and mature about environmental responsibility, we'll learn more and get more respect.

Those fourth graders are also a reminder that so much of caring about the environment is taking personal action. There's a reason why "Be the change you wish to see in the world" is such a popular saying— it's because it works. If we want things to be different, the best place to start is with our very behavior.

Finally, the hugs those kids were glad to offer my friend Erin are a reminder that everybody loves (and sometimes even needs) a little encouragement. The environment is a big issue, but it's not a depressing one. It's so important to encourage each other and to focus on positive changes we *can* make. And like the fourth graders my dad spoke with, one of the places where we can join together to make a big difference is at our schools.

ten steps toward a greener education

There are some very simple things you can do to make your school education kinder to God's creation. Some are purely personal changes, whereas others may take more organization, approval, and support from friends and faculty. Here are just a few:

1. Always write on both sides of your paper. If you use composition paper, make sure to use college-ruled. That one change alone can save hundreds of pieces of paper each year.

Because I'm a lefty, I hate to write on the right-hand sides of notebooks—the binding, wire, or rings get in the way. But that doesn't mean I can't use both sides of the paper. A class usually doesn't take up a whole notebook worth of paper. I can take notes for one subject on the left hand side of each page in the notebook, and then flip the notebook over for another subject, where I can again write on the left side. It works out great. Also: If you have teachers who give handouts with writing only on one side, save them when the class is over and use them in your computer printer or for scrap paper. Most teachers don't mind if an essay is turned in on the other side of a crossed-out science article. (All paper from binders should be recycled at the end of the year.)

You can also use both sides of posters. When teachers take down student posters at the end of the year, they'll usually let you snag the ones with information on only one side so you can use them next year.

2. Walk or ride the bus to school. If neither of these is an option, carpool.

3. If your school isn't already recycling paper and soda cans, you can help get it started. You

just need to get permission to put a cardboard box next to the trash can in each classroom to collect paper. Organize a few friends to help you collect the boxes on a regular basis—preferably friends who have driver's licenses so you can take the paper down to the local recycling center. You should research before starting anything that involves recycling refundable bottles—there are often rules about what kind of collection receptacles can be used for that. At our school, we were only allowed to put barrels inside if they were metal ones specifically made for recycling cans—but even just having plastic barrels outside makes a difference.

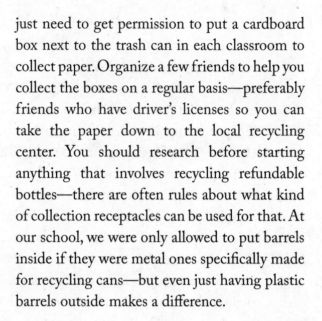

Buy lunch at school? Bring your own drink in a reusable water bottle instead of getting a throwaway carton of juice or milk.

4. Encourage your school to buy two-sided printers for the library or any other place where the printer is used a lot. When it was time to replace the printer in our school library, the head librarian decided to take the leap and get a double-sided printer as well as a converter kit

for the other printer in the library. Together they cost less than $1,400, but the library saved more than three times that in paper costs in the first year alone! Numbers talk: $1,400 invested; $4,500 saved. That printer paid for itself in less than four months, and it'll continue to save money (and trees) for as long as it lasts. If you do a little research and present the numbers to your principal or someone else who has responsibility for making the decision, you're much more likely to get approval.

5. Have your school get recycled paper for all its copiers and printers. Paper that's 100 percent recycled can cost more; if your school isn't willing to go all the way, 30 percent recycled paper costs no more than "regular" paper. Unlike the recycled paper of a decade ago, today's recycled paper will go through printers and copiers fine, and won't cause any more jams or problems than the paper your school is probably using now. Since 30 percent recycled paper costs no more than the paper your school is already buying, it's usually easy to convince your administration to make the switch. However, you might be able to go one step further and combine this project with the printers—using some of the money saved

from double-sided printing to pay for the slightly more expensive 100 percent recycled paper.

6. Along the same lines, paper towels and toilet paper made from recycled paper can usually be bought in bulk at the same price as products made from unrecycled paper. Just a few years ago, this was not the case, but companies are changing their prices so it isn't more expensive to be environmentally friendly. Just get some numbers together, figure out who, you need to talk to, and propose a switch.

7. Schools can purchase other environmentally friendly devices that—like the two-sided printers—will easily pay for themselves over time. It's possible to purchase "energy misers" that can be installed on vending machines to save energy. These cost about $125, and make it so the machine goes into partial hibernation when it's left unused for a long time. (There's a similar device for water fountains that, for instance, can shut off the cooling device overnight.) Just figure out roughly how long it will take for the energy saved to pay for the device. If your school doesn't want to make the investment, but has vending machines where the food doesn't need to be kept cold, see if you

can get permission to turn them off (unplug them) at a certain time after school so they won't be on all night. Maybe you or a friend who lives near the school can be in charge of walking over and unplugging the machines before the school gets locked up for the night, or maybe a custodian can do it as part of the evening routine.

Buy refills for pens instead of disposable ones. Experiment with having only one or two pens or mechanical pencils you really like and see if you lose them less than cheap disposable ones.

Exit lights have to stay on at all times, but they don't have to use as much energy as they're probably using now. Replacing the lights in the signs with LED bulbs will pay for itself in no time and then just keep saving—both energy and money. The same is true of getting compact fluorescents for all the lights in your school.

8. Often, schools don't turn off computers each night. This seems like a simple thing, but

computers that are always left on use a TON
of energy. If your school doesn't already turn
off all its computers, offer to spend 10 minutes
each day turning on all the computers in the
computer lab in the morning and turning them
back off again after school. Contrary to urban
legend, turning computers off once a day will
not harm them; in fact, it will extend their life
as well as greatly reduce the amount of energy
they use.

Get potted plants for a classroom and volunteer to keep
them watered. Not only will they look nice, but they'll also
clean the air for a less polluted indoor environment.

9. Start a collection-and-exchange program at
your school. Our school has a room devoted to
a clothing exchange—students bring in gently
worn clothes they don't wear and can pick up
others they will wear. In the same room is a box
of used three-ring binders that are still in good
shape—students who can't afford binders or
don't wish to purchase a new one can pick one
up anytime. If this kind of permanent exchange
program isn't possible at your school, at least see

if you can do a prom-dress swap. There really aren't too many other occasions to which a prom dress can be worn, and, even if people go to more than one prom during high school, they often don't wear the same dress twice. So collect formal dresses near the end of the year and make them available to other girls to wear. Girls, what are you really going to do with a frilly dress in your closet other than let it hang there? Suits can also be collected, though my experience is that people are more likely to donate dresses. (The suits we did collect were snatched up immediately.) This is a great project for the National Honor Society or another service organization at your school to take on. Before collecting the dresses, make sure you've arranged for a place (a willing teacher's classroom will work) where you can store and display the dresses.

You can also collect used cell phones and printer cartridges. These can be recycled, usually with a refund. Money raised from these collections can be used toward other environmental projects, perhaps to provide the initial investment in things like energy misers or two-sided printers, or to buy trees to plant on the school grounds.

10. Cafeterias are another great place to make environmental changes, though it can be difficult because of regulations and costs. It's often possible to convince school cafeterias to serve vegetarian meals and purchase local food. Getting real plates instead of Styrofoam ones, metal utensils instead of plastic ones, and washable cups instead of disposable ones can be another goal. Some schools even compost their food waste. If you can't convince your school to make big changes, don't give up. You can bring your own lunch in a fabric bag or lunchbox filled with environmentally friendly food choices in washable containers. Although it's great to get other people to change, you can make a difference simply by walking the walk.

wrapping it up

Taking care of God's creation can begin with small steps at your school. Pick your projects, don't lose motivation or get bogged down in bureaucracy, and remember who is guiding your efforts. Everything you do to save the environment is really part of your witness, showing the world how much you love God by respecting the gift of his creation.

Remember, God is on your side. He will help you when you try your hardest to help the world he created. As long as you take advantage of all the resources you have, and work with all the people God provides (Christian and non-Christian), you'll do great.

chapter 9

creation care
and the congregation

I remember running some errands with Mom and Dad a little while ago. Our last stop was the bottle and cans return center. I stayed in the back of the Prius while Mom and Dad brought in our soda cans. Next to our car was the huge truck that picks up cans from this and other recycling centers and drives them to their next step in the journey of being remade and reshipped to grocery stores and repositioned on the shelf.

I must have been in a grouchy mood, because I began to think how small our efforts sometimes seem. Here we are, driving a few blocks out of our way to get to the recycling center. Then there's the center itself: fans going, hundred-watt bulbs glaring, staff driving there every day. I watched several people bring their cans in black plastic garbage bags that are going to be thrown away. And after the cans are counted by the people who work at the center, they'll all go in new plastic bags. These bags will be thrown into a truck and driven somewhere so the aluminum can be melted down and formed into new cans—all of which takes a lot of energy. Then, after the cans are filled, they're packed by 12s and 24s into cardboard boxes, which are then redistributed all across the country. People drive to a store, purchase these refrigerated cans, and the whole process starts all over again. And for what? So we can have artificially colored, carbonated sugar water.

How can we ever save the planet with these little acts of conservation?

Most environmentalists would just give me the facts—it takes ten times more energy to produce a new aluminum can than to recycle a can, so the energy savings are enormous. Other environmentalists would remind me that something is better than nothing. Still others would say that if people simply cooperate, then we could save the planet.

I agree with these environmentalists, to a point. I believe we need to get our facts right, to take small steps, and to cooperate with others working toward the same goal. But I also think we need something else, something bigger, in order to save the planet. We need God.

When the disciples asked Jesus how a person could be saved, he responded, "With human beings this is impossible, but with God all things are possible" (Matthew 19:26). The same is true about saving our environment.

I don't think we will ever save the planet simply by recycling soda cans. But I do think God can and will use our efforts to save the environment to do mighty things throughout the world.

Make up information sheets about recycling and God's love for the planet and hand them out at the door as people enter before Sunday services or as people leave after worship.

Don't get me wrong: Christians need to recycle. We can't just sit back and wait for God to miraculously restore the environment to its former glory. In fact, I believe we Christians need to pray incessantly that the Holy Spirit would fill us with a holy fire that leads us to take the environment and conservation seriously. But I believe we'll only make a real difference when we see caring for the earth as part of what God calls us to.

If our motivation is lowering the price of gas, we will not succeed. If our focus is on preserving the rapidly melting icecaps, cleaning up the skies so we can see the stars, or preventing natural disasters brought on by climate change, we will most likely fail. If the five-cent deposit we get for returning our soda bottles is all that motivates us, we will get our couple of dollars but we probably won't get a markedly cleaner world. As important as it is to provide a cleaner, safer world to keep the next generation of children from environmental harm, I believe the church will find the power to transform the world only if we are motivated by the higher calling of pleasing our Lord.

let it begin—with me

At the first church I attended, we sang, "Let There Be Peace on Earth," at the end of each service. I like the song because it asks God to make us his instruments for change. The song doesn't say, "Let the government seek peace," or, "Let all guns in the world malfunction at this point in time." No, it says, "Let there be peace on earth, and let it begin with *me*." The next verse makes it clear we aren't asking for peace to come in a week or in a year or in our lifetime. No, it says, "Let there be peace on earth; let this be the moment *now*."

The environmental movement needs to begin with me, with you, with all of us—the body of Christ. The church cannot put off caring for the planet any longer. We need to start now.

We need to pray. We need to ask that God would let change begin with us. We need to ask, as God's children, to be used in powerful ways to protect his planet. Rather than focusing on the perceived hypocrisy or futility of conservation efforts, we need to focus on God—the One who made this earth and can use our efforts to change and preserve it.

15 steps toward an earth-friendly church

If the environment is going to be saved, I truly believe churches will have to be the home base. Local churches will have to take a stand for the world God created and loves. But before we can expect the rest of the world to change its ways, the church needs to clean up its own act.

There are many practical steps your church can take to have a more positive impact on the environment:

1. Change the light bulbs in the church to energy-efficient ones. We are called to be "a

light unto the world." Let's make sure it's an energy-efficient light!

Have stained-glass windows in your church? Check out getting heavy drapes to cover them when the sanctuary is not in use to save on heating and cooling.

2. Set up a box to collect church bulletins as people exit the church so the bulletins can be recycled. Even better, encourage people to share bulletins so fewer are made each week or reduce the bulletin to fewer pages. If your church bulletin includes announcements, maybe you could print fewer announcement pages and encourage families to share them. You can also recycle in the church kitchen. Set up boxes for cans, plastic, and paper, and bring them to the recycling center on a regular basis.

3. Just because your church has a "coffee hour" after church doesn't mean you have to serve coffee. Consider changing the beverage served—or at least switch to organic, shade-grown coffee. Yes, it does cost a little more, but you will be saving agricultural land from

erosion and pesticides, and helping the people who tend and harvest the coffee.

4. Organize a church garden. Start small and invite volunteers from the church to help plant, weed, and harvest. If your church sponsors a soup kitchen, fresh produce will be a welcome addition. If not, you can probably find a local homeless shelter or soup kitchen that would be glad to have the food. A church garden is also a great way to invite people outside the church who might be interested in gardening or community service to become involved. Think about how many parables Jesus told about planting seed, gardening, and vineyards. A garden is a perfect object lesson.

5. If your church doesn't already have one, start an exchange program. Just having a simple bulletin board where people can indicate what they need and what people have to give away or share can prevent a lot of unnecessary purchases. If possible, set up a way people can share tools. We don't all need to have our own personal lawnmower, weed whacker, table saw, bicycle pump, snow blower, and pickup truck. Even if just three families started sharing a single lawnmower, that would mean there

are two fewer lawnmowers that need to be manufactured and purchased in this world.

6. Encourage your church to get an energy audit to see how its energy efficiency can be improved. Many church buildings can save substantial amounts of energy through simple changes, such as more insulation, roof fans, and curtains. If the church is heated during the winter or cooled in the summer, just a few degrees on the thermostat can save a lot of energy.

7. Hold a church yard sale. The fewer things we have, the less distraction in our lives and the more time we have to spend with God. The money raised can be used to make the church more energy efficient, or can be given to church outreach, missionaries, or charities.

8. Bring in an outside speaker to speak to the church about environmental issues, or see if there's anyone in the congregation who can speak on stewardship. If your church does adult Sunday school or other small groups, consider focusing a class on God-centered environmentalism and what group members can do to improve their own impact on the ecosystem.

9. Creation-care issues need prayer. Hold prayer meetings for the people most affected by the environmental changes occurring today. Pray that people in your church and throughout the world would hear God's call to take positive action. Pray for wisdom to know what to do and the strength to carry out God's will.

See if your church could use a little more insulation. Present to your pastor information on the amount of money that would be saved in heating and cooling costs over the years. Offer for your youth group to do fund-raisers to offset the initial installation costs.

10. Plant trees. Like a community garden, this is a great outreach opportunity—as well as a way to care for the earth. Either plant saplings around the church or see if there is a local park or other public place where new trees would be welcomed.

11. Organize carpools to and from church. If there are many people who come from one area (such as a college campus or retirement home), see if the church can arrange a van or bus to

bring them all to church instead of their driving separately.

12. Share your church building with other organizations. With a little flexibility and planning, multiple congregations can even share a single church building on Sundays. Soup kitchens and community lectures can be held during the week. As long as the building is there, it might as well be put to good use. Remember: The church is not a building; it's a body of believers.

Get involved in Sunday school. Offer to lead a class of kids with a few of your friends and teach about God's love for nature. Leave them with practical ways they can live it out—make recycling bins or have them decorate Bible verses about the environment they can hang up at home.

13. Turn off the electronic devices in the church when they're not in use. Don't leave computers, electronic musical equipment, or lights on all week. This includes refrigerators: If there are refrigerators that are used for church suppers or special occasions but are otherwise empty,

unplug them. Prop the doors open so fungus doesn't grow, and just plug them back in when they are needed.

14. Get all the hyper seventh graders in youth group together and see if you can light the whole church for a year by playing the "who can pedal the most on the electric generator bike?" game. Just kidding. But I bet the youth group leaders would like the idea.

15. Make sure the cleaning products used at the church are safe for the environment (no phosphates). Also, use paper towels and toilet paper made from recycled paper, and install water savers for the toilets at the church (a gallon jug filled with water or a few bricks in the toilet tank is a low-cost solution).

wrapping it up

Obviously, you can't make all these changes on your own. You will need the approval of your pastor and other superiors in the church in order to execute many of these plans. But you will also need the support of the congregation, and, more importantly, your friends. It is not your pastor's generation that we need to change. It is not the generation before him. It is our generation that needs to care about the environment from God's perspective. Get your youth group involved. Organize as many events and changes as you can utilizing one of your best assets: your peers. If we raise the bar, others will rise to the occasion. If our congregations can see that we really do believe in protecting the planet God created, that we really do think conservation is a biblical practice, I believe that they will respect and support us in our efforts. If we bring the passion and the dedication, they will help us with the finances, with the rides, and with the infrastructure needed for our ventures.

chapter 10

back to the future

I've always been fascinated by the rings on trees and how they represent the different stages of a tree's life. Some rings are thick, showing periods of prosperity and health, while others are not as wide, indicating a more difficult time. Yet all mark the passage of time.

Even as I've been working on this book, time has gone by. I started writing this book when I was a junior in high school—my whole life in front of me. Now I'm in my sophomore year of college—still pretty much my whole life in front of me, minus a couple of years.

One of the most amazing things for me about going to college was that so much more of *everything* was up to me—what I ate, where I went, and what I did. I've talked throughout this book about a number of environmental habits that I developed from my parents in my home growing up. Obviously, I held onto a lot of those when I arrived at college. But I realized that my environmental impact there was even more up to me than it ever had been before. At home, my mom and dad had a large influence on my eco-sensitivity and environmental impact. But in the dorm, it was up to me. Would I get a fluorescent or incandescent bulb to put in my bedside lamp? Would I use the dryer or find a way to continue hanging my clothes up to dry? Would I try not to use air conditioning or would I get used to having it so readily available?

Get a traditional phone instead of a cordless set for your dorm room—they use much less energy.

For me, after completing high school, college was the next ring in my "tree." For you, it might be something different—employment or an intern year, maybe. Whatever it is, though, transitioning from high school to the next stage of your life will mean more responsibilities—and more choices. How thick is the next ring on your tree going to be? Will it be a year in which you and the earth will prosper? Are you going to grow and nurture your eco-healthy, green lifestyle?

Take only as much as you're sure you can eat in the cafeteria. You can always go back for seconds. And take only a plate instead of both plate and tray when you go through the cafeteria line. It'll be one less thing to go through the dishwasher!

It took a while to get into my own environmental groove at college. After some troubleshooting, I found

Does your dorm room have air-conditioning? Try using a fan instead. And in the winter, pile on extra blankets at night so you can turn down the heat. Make sure your roommate has another comforter, too!

out what worked and what I had time for. I discovered that hanging my clothes up to dry was actually just as fast as waiting for an automatic dryer on Sunday night—the time when everyone realizes they have nothing clean to wear the next day to class. My dorm has a recycling bin in the trash room on each floor, and after the first few weeks when I found myself walking down there a couple of times each day, I found it easier to keep a milk crate under my bed to collect my recyclables and then dump the milk crate into the larger bin about once a week.

Instead of using the overhead light, use small, energy-efficient lamps when studying at your desk or on your bed.

My school is still getting into green issues, so I spent much of my freshman year figuring out who

Do you have some kind of frequent schoolwide meetings—chapel or assemblies? See if you can get an environmental speaker to come and talk to your school about being green.

had a passion for positive change and how I could join efforts with them to get the ball rolling. At the end of my freshman year, we started a student chapter of

Christians in Conservation/A Rocha USA. (A Rocha is an international conservation organization—you'll find more info about them at the back of the book.) My sophomore year has meant getting more involved and taking on a leadership role.

> Find out if there's an environmental group on campus—and then get involved. If there's no club in existence, consider starting one yourself.

But the biggest contributors by far toward a healthy "ring" for me in college have been the other girls in my dorm. My resident director is an amazing

> If your school doesn't have an extensive recycling program, get permission to put boxes on each floor of the dorms at the end of the semester, for recycling paper when everyone is cleaning out their binders. Make sure to have some friends to help you distribute and collect the boxes.

woman who somehow finds time to coordinate recycling efforts with the town where our college is located, while still fulfilling her full-time job of loving, teaching, and nurturing us all to grow. My "big sister," Felice, who was assigned to me when I first came to Asbury, has also encouraged my passion for being green. I'm such

---

Getting things for your dorm room? Check out organic bedding and get dishes from yard sales or Goodwill.

---

a "doer"—but Felice's more contemplative approach to the state of the ecosystem has helped me think more deeply about the issue. Whether it's planting basil in a pot on her windowsill or drinking organic tea, she always seems to be living what she's thinking.

Share a printer with your roommate instead of buying two. You can take turns buying the paper and ink. And always use recycled paper.

And, of course, there's my roommate. If you decide to go to college, I hope you'll love your roommate as much as I love mine. Jenny is perfect. She's thoughtful, she's funny, she's bright. I could go on for pages and pages about how amazing my roomie is. But one of the things I love most about her is that she puts up with me and my quirky ways—she even encourages some of them! When I challenge her to a race in the rain, I love the fact that she doesn't look at me like I'm crazy—she changes into her shorts and running shoes! I love that she puts her used paper in my milk crate recycling receptacle. I love that instead of being weirded out by my love for shopping at Goodwill, she actually enjoys spending a Saturday with me going to all the thrift stores nearby and picking out outfits.

> Organize a cleanup of a road, stream, or path that is littered near your campus.

A lot of college is figuring out what kind of person you want to be once you graduate. It's a great place to foster environmentally sustainable habits in your life. It's a great place to figure out that it's easy being green.

wrapping it up

When I was a child, one of my favorite books was *The Little Engine That Could.* The story is about a big train that breaks down while carrying a load of toys and other good things to children who live on the other side of a mountain. The broken-down engine asks several other passing trains for help, but they are either unable or unwilling. Finally, he sees a tiny blue engine, and asks that much smaller engine if he'll pull the shipment of good things to the children on the other side of the mountain. The little train looks up at that huge mountain, and isn't sure he's up to the task. But finally he decides to give it a go. And all the way up the hill, our little hero puffs, "I think I can. I think I can. I

Do the dorms have separate electric meters? Ask the RDs if you could organize a competition between the dorms to see which one can use the least amount of energy.

think I can."

Like that little train, we may feel like there's a huge mountain standing between us and the greener world we long for. But Jesus had a few words for us about mountains. In Matthew 17:20, he says, "If you have faith as small as a mustard seed, you can say to this mountain, 'Move from here to there,' and it will move.

Nothing will be impossible for you."

With faith in God, nothing is impossible. Living a green life is within the reach of every one of us. I think you can. God thinks you can.

When the children from the next "valley," from the next generation, see us and the world we pass on to them, my hope is that they'll see a generation that was green. My hope is that they'll see a generation that took its choices seriously, that placed its faith in God, and found the strength to climb the highest mountain.

My hope is that they'll see a little generation that did.

appendix a

the living word: environmental scripture references

"In the beginning God created the heavens and the earth…God saw all that he had made, and it was very good."

Genesis 1:1, 31

"I now establish my covenant with you and with your descendants after you and with every living creature that was with you—the birds, the livestock and all the wild animals, all those that came out of the ark with you—every living creature on earth."

Genesis 9:9-10

"Follow my decrees and be careful to obey my laws, and you will live safely in the land. Then the land will

yield its fruit, and you will eat your fill and live there in safety...The land must not be sold permanently, because the land is mine and you reside in my land as foreigners and strangers."
Leviticus 25:18-19, 23

"To the Lord your God belong the heavens, even the highest heavens, the earth and everything in it."
Deuteronomy 10:14

"...for the Lord your God is God in heaven above and on the earth below."
Joshua 2:11b

"You alone are the Lord. You made the heavens, even the highest heavens, and all their starry host, the earth and all that is on it, the seas and all that is in them. You give life to everything, and the multitudes of heaven worship you."
Nehemiah 9:6

"The heavens declare the glory of God; the skies proclaim the work of his hands. Day after day they pour forth speech; night after night they display knowledge. They have no speech, they use no words; no sound is

heard from them. Yet their voice goes out into all the earth, their words to the ends of the world."
Psalm 19:1-4

"The earth is the Lord's, and everything in it, the world, and all who live in it."
Psalm 24:1

"Sing to the Lord a new song; sing to the Lord, all the earth...Let the heavens rejoice, let the earth be glad; let the sea resound, and all that is in it. Let the fields be jubilant, and everything in them; let all the trees of the forest sing for joy."
Psalm 96:1, 11-12

"How many are your works, Lord! In wisdom you made them all; the earth is full of your creatures. There is the sea, vast and spacious, teeming with creatures beyond number—living things both large and small."
Psalm 104:24-25

"The desert and the parched land will be glad; the wilderness will rejoice and blossom. Like the crocus, it will burst into bloom; it will rejoice greatly and shout

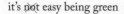

for joy...Water will gush forth in the wilderness and
streams in the desert."

Isaiah 35:1-2, 6

"Who has measured the waters in the hollow of his
hand, or with the breadth of his hand marked off the
heavens? Who has held the dust of the earth in a basket,
or weighed the mountains on the scales and the hills in
a balance?...Lift up your eyes and look to the heavens:
Who created all these? He who brings out the starry
host one by one, and calls them each by name."

Isaiah 40:12, 26

"The wild animals honor me, the jackals and the owls,
because I provide water in the wilderness."

Isaiah 43:20

"Hear the word of the Lord, you Israelites, because
the Lord has a charge to bring against you who live
in the land: 'There is no faithfulness, no love, no
acknowledgment of God in the land. There is only
cursing, lying and murder, stealing and adultery; they
break all bounds, and bloodshed follows bloodshed.
Because of this the land dries up, and all who live in it
waste away; the beasts of the field, the birds in the sky
and the fish in the sea are swept away.'"

Hosea 4:1-3

"Through him all things were made; without him nothing was made that has been made."

John 1:3

"The Son is the image of the invisible God, the firstborn over all creation. For in him all things were created: things in heaven and on earth, visible and invisible... For God was pleased to have all his fullness dwell in him, and through him to reconcile to himself all things, whether things on earth or things in heaven, by making peace through his blood, shed on the cross."

Colossians 1:15-16, 19-20

"You are worthy, our Lord and God, to receive glory and honor and power, for you created all things, and by your will they were created and have their being."

Revelation 4:11

"The nations were angry, and your wrath has come. The time has come for judging the dead, and for rewarding your servants the prophets and your people who revere your name, both great and small—and for destroying those who destroy the earth."

Revelation 11:18

appendix b

greening your library: cool environmental books to check out

True Green: 100 Everyday Ways You Can Contribute to a Healthier Planet, Kim McKay and Jenny Bonnin

Okay, I'll admit it: I still like books with pictures. *True Green* is a quick and interesting read filled with practical, easy tips and, yup, lots of pictures. It contains many interesting statistics and is formatted in an accessible way so you can find the information you want quickly. It's a great book to borrow from the library and flip through for a few eco-friendly tips—I'd highly recommend it to readers at all levels of environmentalism.

Saving God's Green Earth: Rediscovering the Church's Responsibility to Environmental Stewardship, Tri Robinson

Is your church interested in greening up? In a simple, easy-to-read voice, author and pastor Tri Robinson makes the case for Christian environmental responsibility and shares the story of how his large church was transformed into the vanguard of the Christian conservation movement.

Serve God, Save the Planet: A Christian Call to Action, J. Matthew Sleeth, MD (a.k.a. my dad)

Of course, I'm a little partial to this book. In fact, I wouldn't hesitate to say it's the best book on Christian environmentalism out there—and that's not *just* because my dad wrote it. In a loving and engaging manner, Dad shares the story of his journey from ER doctor to full-time environmentalist. I've seen the transformational power his story has had on people from all walks of life. If you're only going to read one book on the environment, make it this one.

The Little Green Handbook: Seven Trends Shaping the Future of Our Planet, Ron Nielsen

Don't let the title fool you: This book's not exactly *little.* But if you're into statistics and really want to learn about the world we live in today, it's just the thing for you. Well organized and researched, *The Little Green Handbook* is a great resource for in-depth study—or just to have around to look up a thing or two.

The Man Who Planted Trees, Jean Giono

This is a short, inspirational story about the power one person has to change the world. *The Man Who Planted Trees* tells the story of how one simple peasant transformed a desolate region, one seed at a time. Read it through and you'll want to go out and plant your own forest!

Babysitting or teaching a Sunday school class? There are a few great picture books with environmental messages that you might want to get from the library and read aloud. Check out *Just a Dream* by Chris Van Allsburg, *The Giving Tree* by Shel Silverstein, and *The Lorax* by Dr. Seuss.

appendix c

picture this: movies you might want to see

Affluenza

This one-hour film produced by PBS explores the "epidemic of affluence" that is spreading across the United States. It is a great resource to help middle-class Americans living in a nation of unprecedented wealth examine the social and environmental costs of our lifestyle.

Winged Migration

The beautiful cinematography alone is more than enough to make this documentary film worthwhile. But it's also a fascinating study of the migration of different bird species. A well-done and engaging film that offers a "bird's eye view" of the amazing wonder of God's creation.

The Great Warming

Here's an informational work about global warming that presents the facts in an understandable manner. A lot of the details are focused on Canada, but it contains a great deal of universal principles and information.

An Inconvenient Truth

I don't know your political views, but I don't think the facts about global warming change whether you support the person presenting them or not. Even if you don't agree with everything Al Gore says, this is probably the most frequently viewed and talked about documentary ever made about the critical issue of climate change.

Kilowatt Ours

This is one of my favorite films about the environment. It focuses on where energy comes from—with a special focus on the southeastern United States—and then explains how to cut down personal energy use and what others are doing to go to green power. *Kilowatt Ours* is educational and inspirational—a perfect combination.

appendix d

getting involved: a few organizations that might interest you

Restoring Eden (www.restoringeden.org) is a Christian environmental organization that seeks to make "your heart bigger, your hands dirtier, your voice stronger for God's creation." Started by Peter Illyn, the ministry has chapters on many college campuses. Look them up on the Web to see how you can get involved or start a chapter at the school you want to attend.

A Rocha (www.arocha.org) is the largest international Christian conservation organization in the world. A Rocha, which means "The Rock" in Portuguese, offers great volunteer positions at field centers around the world as well as a growing branch in the United States.

Floresta (www.floresta.org) is a Christian nonprofit working to reverse deforestation and poverty in the world, by empowering the rural poor. Floresta has planted more than 2.5 million trees around the world, and educates people in poverty about sustainable agricultural practices.

Sierra Student Coalition (www.ssc.org) is the student branch of the Sierra Club. The Sierra Club is not specifically Christian, but I still believe in what it's doing all the way. The group now has chapters on more than 250 campuses across the country—and loves to have both high school and college-age students involved.

Many people think teenagers aren't capable of much. But Zach Hunter is proving those people wrong. He's only fifteen, but he's working to end slavery in the world—and he's making changes that affect millions of people. Find out how Zach is making a difference and how you can make changes in the things that you see wrong with our world.

Be the Change
Your Guide to Freeing Slaves and Changing the World
Zach Hunter
RETAIL $9.99
ISBN 0-310-27756-6

Visit www.invertbooks.com or your local bookstore.

LIFE AND FAITH CAN BE HARD WHEN YOU'RE IN MIDDLE SCHOOL. BUT THIS BOOK GIVES YOU ALL THE TIPS AND SECRETS YOU NEED TO REALLY GRASP YOUR FAITH AND KEEP HOLD OF IT.

My Faith
Middle School Survival Series
Kurt Johnston & Mark Oestreicher

RETAIL $9.99
ISBN 0-310-27382-X

EVERYTHING IS CHANGING—INCLUDING THE WAY YOUR FAMILY INTERACTS. THIS BOOK WILL GIVE YOU SECRETS AND TIPS TO HELP MAKE YOUR FAMILY EVEN BETTER AND SURVIVE THE CHANGES THAT COME ALONG WITH MIDDLE SCHOOL.

My Family
Middle School Survival Series
Kurt Johnston & Mark Oestreicher

RETAIL $9.99
ISBN 0-310-27430-3

Visit www.invertbooks.com or your local bookstore.

If you've ever wondered if God is really there and listening,
if you're good enough, or what's so great about heaven,
you're not alone. We all have had personal questions, but
the answers are often harder to come by. In this book, you'll
discover how to navigate your big questions, and what the
answers mean for your life and faith.

Living with Questions
Dale Fincher
RETAIL $9.99
ISBN 0-310-27664-0

Visit www.invertbooks.com or your local bookstore.

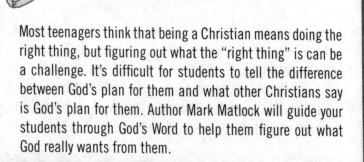

Most teenagers think that being a Christian means doing the right thing, but figuring out what the "right thing" is can be a challenge. It's difficult for students to tell the difference between God's plan for them and what other Christians say is God's plan for them. Author Mark Matlock will guide your students through God's Word to help them figure out what God really wants from them.

What Does God Want from Me?
Understanding God's Desire for Your Life
Mark Matlock
RETAIL $9.99
ISBN 0-310-25815-4

invert

Visit www.invertbooks.com or your local bookstore.

Love This! contains real-life stories of people like you who've found ways to love their neighbors. It will challenge you to make a difference in your world by loving people who are often ignored or unloved—the homeless, the addicted, the elderly, those of different races, even your enemies—and show you tangible ways you can demonstrate that love.

Love This!
Learning to Make It a Way of Life, Not Just a Word
Andy Braner
RETAIL $12.99
ISBN 0-310-27380-3

Visit www.invertbooks.com or your local bookstore.

What gives life meaning? Is it money, sex, power, knowledge, love? Ecclesiastes is about a king who tried all of the above and came to a radical conclusion about how life should be lived. *Living a Life That Matters* helps you make sense of Solomon's experiences, leads you to meaning in your own life, and gives you the tools to help your friends do the same.

Living a Life that Matters
Lessons from Solomon—the man who tried everything
Chris Lyon and Mark Matlock
RETAIL $9.99
ISBN 0-310-25816-2

Visit www.invertbooks.com or your local bookstore.